the first
six weeks

the first
six weeks

The tried-and-tested guide that shows you
how to have a happy, healthy, sleeping baby

Midwife Cath
FOREWORD BY DR LEN KLIMAN

ALLEN&UNWIN
SYDNEY·MELBOURNE·AUCKLAND·LONDON

First published in 2016

Copyright © Cathryn Curtin 2016

Allen & Unwin
83 Alexander Street
Crows Nest NSW 2065
Australia
Phone: (61 2) 8425 0100
Email: info@allenandunwin.com
Web: www.allenandunwin.com

Cataloguing-in-Publication details are available
from the National Library of Australia
www.trove.nla.gov.au

ISBN 978 1 74343 996 8

Set in 12.5/18.75 pt Fairfield by Bookhouse, Sydney
Printed and bound in Australia by Griffin Press

10 9 8

Author's note

I use 'he' when referring to the baby in the book because my own baby was a boy. I also refer to babies as 'he' because so many new parents do not want to know the sex of their child (and I know) so I have trained myself to say 'he'. No offence is intended to baby girls!

There are also many types of families, and I recognise that many people parent alone. Then there are families with same-sex parents or who live within an extended family. Please read this book by adapting it as necessary to your situation. I am aware of the different family structures, and the challenges unique to each.

*Dedicated to my loving parents Doreen and Jack Curtin,
and my wonderful son Lachlan Curtin-Corr.*

Foreword by
Dr Len Kliman

As an obstetrician and gynaecologist I have worked with Cathryn Curtin for over 30 years in family birth centres, obstetric units and birth suites.

At our first meeting, Cath was in charge of the Family Birth Centre at St Andrew's Hospital in Melbourne, Australia. This was when I became acquainted with Cath's unique midwifery and interpersonal skills. Our working relationship continued when Cath took over the mantle as the midwife in charge of the obstetric unit and labour ward at Masada Hospital in Melbourne.

When I established the Chemical Dependency Clinic for the management of women with drug abuse problems in pregnancy at the Royal Women's Hospital Cath came to work for us as our principal midwife. After that long journey into a difficult and challenging but rewarding area of obstetrics, Cath has been the midwife in my private practice ever since, and continues in this role today.

In my practice Cath has looked after patients antenatally, been intimately involved in patient education and, more importantly, has attended to my patients postnatally as a midwife adviser, maternal and child health practitioner. More importantly, she is a confidant to most of my patients. Every week in my private practice a patient will say to me during her postnatal visit, 'Cath literally saved my life.'

Although we all focus on antenatal and intrapartum care for our patients, the really complicated, exhausting and challenging part of motherhood really starts when a new mother takes her new baby home. This is when Cath's advice and care is outstanding.

There is no baby Cath can't get on to a breast, where patients have previously found breastfeeding and attaching the baby to the breast impossible. There is no baby Cath can't settle, when new mothers are finding it impossible to calm and feed their newborn and get some well-needed sleep.

I am delighted that Cath is putting her outstanding abilities into print so that a wider audience can reap the benefits of her commonsense and rational approach to the challenges—and joys—of motherhood.

Foreword by Bec Judd

Cath Curtin is a like a guardian angel who roams this earth protecting and nurturing parents and brand new bubs from the craziness of the newborn phase.

Nothing, and I mean *nothing*, can prepare you for the tornado that is new parenthood. God help me if I hadn't had Cath to show me the way. A shoulder to cry on and an ear to listen to new parents' many obsessive topics of conversation (which I'm sure in her 40 years of midwifery and maternal and child health nurse career she has heard *every single day*).

'He poohed twice, he's pulling away at my breast, urghhh my nipples hurt, I think he's got reflux, he woke at 10, 2, 4 and 6, he's got a fever, is green poo OK? What about yellow?' Yep—never did Cath's attention waiver, her focus diminish; nor did she grow tired of my incessant questions.

Cath has a knack for babies. You know, one of those people who just have IT. The baby screams all day and as soon as

Cath waltzes into the room and picks him up he turns from nightmare gremlin into a smiling (assassin), happy, gooing, gahhing baby? Yep, that's her.

With a focus on the mother, father and baby, Cath offers a no-nonsense, logical and commonsense approach to parenthood that works. There's no denying that if the mother is happy and settled, then in turn, the baby will be too.

With my first child Oscar I have been very open in saying that I didn't enjoy the first six weeks of his life. Of course I loved him and would definitely take a bullet for him, but I can hand-on-the-heart say that I wasn't having the time of my life. Hmmmm, was it bad that I was wishing I was still pregnant so I could have some quiet time with my husband and go to cafes whenever I wanted to? Yes, it took a while to transition from being a self-involved couple to PARENTS and Cath seemed to know exactly what I was thinking and feeling, and guided me through that tricky time. 'It gets better, I promise,' she would say, and she was so right.

From dealing with my mastitis, Oscar's reflux, his inability to sleep during the day and my guilt associated with finding breastfeeding too hard that I just wanted to formula-feed him, Cath made me feel in control and never judged me along the way. She empowers the mother and I am forever grateful to her as my family and I have always been happy, healthy and well slept, right from the beginning.

Thank you, Cath. xox

Contents

Author's note   v
Foreword by Dr Len Kliman   vii
Foreword by Bec Judd   ix
Introduction   xiii

 1   Why the first six weeks are important   1
 2   Getting ready   10
 3   Happy birthday   20
 4   The first few days ... and into the first week   59
 5   Week two   127
 6   Week three   156
 7   Week four   180
 8   Week five   204
 9   Week six   223
10   Beyond six weeks   256

Seeking help   271
Acknowledgements   275
Index   279

Introduction

Working with pregnant women, helping babies come into the world and guiding their parents in the early years of their children's lives has been my life's work. I feel extremely fortunate to have always worked in a field that I love.

I have cared for pregnant women from the ages of fourteen to 49-plus, and can say it remains a privilege to be allowed into the lives of so many families. It is incredible to be present at a birth. Ten thousand babies later, I can say I've seen it all, but I *never* get tired of seeing babies born and watching them bond with their new parents.

I have wanted to be a midwife for as long as I can remember. I have been reading medical books since I was eight, so from an early age I not only had an innate understanding of how the human body worked but also realised that I wanted to work in medicine at some level for the rest of my life. As the youngest of eight children I had plenty of babies around me—21 nieces and nephews were all born after I turned thirteen, so I had heaps of hands-on experience handling, feeding, bathing, holding and babysitting.

My mother Doreen was an amazingly strong and wise woman and mother, and with my father Jack, an intelligent man of great humour and sensitivity, taught by example. Theirs was an uncomplicated and loving parenting, a true partnership that successfully raised us with love, amazing life experiences such as travel, and lots of fun.

I began training as a nurse in 1975 at St Vincent's Hospital in Melbourne, then as a midwife in 1979 at the Mercy Hospital in East Melbourne. During that year as a student midwife I delivered two very special baby girls.

The first baby I ever delivered was called Jane, and a few months later I delivered another little girl named Renée. Fast forward to 2013, I was lucky enough to help both Jane and then Renée during their pregnancies, births and early parenting. Jane is mother to Henry and Leila, and Renée to Charlotte and baby Oliver. It's been a wonderful experience to deliver my babies' babies, and to continue to be in their lives to this day.

Those early days as a midwife involved hours upon hours of learning the art of midwifery, listening and watching and caring for women, and guiding them in labour. I have always been acutely aware that when caring for a woman in labour I have two lives in my hands at any one time.

I was thrilled to win a scholarship to study Maternal and Child Health (MCH) full time when I was still a young midwife, and got to learn all about a baby's health and development from birth to school age.

I have learnt a lot from observing newborn babies, and am still amazed by their primitive reflexes and their will to live. My training has proved invaluable in teaching today's new parents about babies' sleep, feeding, development, how toddlers think and behave, why some sleep, why others don't—and how to get them to do so. I also keep up with the latest readings within my field, and am fortunate to work closely with fantastic obstetricians and paediatricians.

I have worked with obstetrician and gynaecologist Dr Len Kliman for over 30 years. Eleven years ago, Len and I set out to create a new model of care within his private practice in East Melbourne. We had both worked with pregnant women for decades, and believed it could be done so much better, especially with the continuity of care after the baby's birth. All patients see Len during their pregnancy and he is present at the birth. They also have access to my services before and after the birth of their baby, for everything from counselling to breastfeeding support and postnatal breastfeeding, parenting support and care.

I am passionate about promoting a 'happy mother'. If the mother in the family is well and happy, everyone is.

❦

The 'Midwife Cath' website began when the first iPhone was released while I was in New York. I sat in the Apple auditorium listening to how these amazing new phones worked and how something called 'applications' could be made. I knew instantly this platform would be an excellent way to help educate new parents around the world. I was becoming frustrated with all the confusing and conflicting information new parents were being bombarded with in their early days in the hospital, as well as through the numerous well-written and well-intentioned but misguided parenting books. It didn't help that this message was being reinforced at the community level.

The information overload starts in pregnancy. Google and girlfriends can confuse a new mother as they pass on information or tell you what they did successfully with their babies. Often your friends have had only one or two babies, so their experience cannot predict how *your* baby will feed, sleep, play or develop. Your baby is unique.

Then you have a plethora of professionals giving you conflicting advice . . . not to mention the grocer, your neighbour and even strangers in the supermarket coming up to you, touching your belly and offering advice.

Too many new parents were becoming unnecessarily anxious, worrying too much about minor issues.

I know from experience that parents are physically and emotionally overwhelmed after the birth of their beautiful baby, which is why I spend much of my time talking to new parents through those early weeks. This book comes from those 10,000 babies, and the practical thoughts and ideas that have worked and helped new parents.

I do not see myself as a baby whisperer or a guru, but a nurse, midwife and maternal and child health nurse dedicated to the health and welfare of new parents and their babies.

My approach is very simple: I teach parenting in a pragmatic and realistic way that makes it easy for new parents to put it into practice at home. I am also a mum and have practised what I preach—with great success! Always, I hear my mum's voice saying to me, 'Have a shower first thing in the morning, be positive, feed your baby, love your baby, talk to your child with respect, work hard, and let the rest happen.'

I am currently going through the newborn phase for the third time: I have a six-year-old, twin four-year-olds and now a four-week-old. This time has been by far the most enjoyable experience as I have finally figured out what works for me. It's not sleeping when the baby sleeps; it's not asking others to fold my laundry and it's not swaddling. All these are good things, but they are not what's making this experience better. I have finally figured out that my happiness is essential for my newborn's happiness and that of my family. It is a cliché, but there is a lot of truth in 'happy mum, happy baby'.

This mantra has allowed me to say 'no' to visitors wanting to come when all I want to do is lie on the couch and watch TV. It's allowed me to let my baby sleep on me when I feel like a cuddle and not worry about 'making a rod for my own back', and it's allowed me to make different feeding choices than previously.

And guess what? My baby is the calmest one I've had. This is the first time I am not wishing away these early weeks—something I never believed I would say.

We are taught to meet babies' needs through many practical techniques—routines, swaddling, feeding patterns. But our emotional state is just as important. Giving mothers permission to put their needs first allows us to relate to our babies from a place of contentment—a more enjoyable outcome for all involved.

SARA

1

Why the first six weeks are important

Remember when you had your scans during pregnancy? You worried and thought, 'I hope the baby's OK.' Then after the scans were normal you'd leave the doctor's office happy, before worrying about what might happen *next* week. You don't know what you don't know.

This is parenting. That feeling of slight worry doesn't leave, and that's how we feel all the time. It's OK to worry about your children, but you need to come to terms with how you feel about parenting, and not get too anxious and worry about 'what could happen next week' or 'if the baby doesn't sleep tonight'. This ruminating prevents you staying in the present and being responsive to your baby in the here and now.

Instead, learn to take it as it comes. If you have a well baby, look on him as healthy and try not to problem-solve what is 'wrong' with him. I will tell you many times during this book that *your baby cannot be sick and well at the same time*. This is *your* baby, and there exists a unique bond between you as mother and child. You know more than you think.

The first six weeks after birth are some of the happiest days you'll ever experience and also the hardest. Nothing can prepare you for the sleep deprivation, the tears, the love and the confusion. These first six weeks establish your life of parenting. I know there is much you can do in these first weeks to set you up to have a baby who sleeps for five to six hours from 11 pm, which becomes the basis of you feeling happy, confident and positive as a parent.

So many 'things' happen in the first six weeks that need attention. You may require a professional to help you through some of these issues, to problem-solve what is causing concern and then to receive ongoing support and treatment when necessary. Things like recovering from birth, establishing breastfeeding, pain, wound infection, constipation, raw and uncontrollable emotions, breast engorgement, a baby with gastric reflux or cow's milk protein allergy, a crying baby, a noisy baby, sleep deprivation, sore, cracked and bleeding nipples, mastitis and then immunisations at six weeks . . . It sounds like fun, doesn't it!

I know if you can get through these first six weeks with a baby who is sleeping a good stretch overnight and you feel well and supported, you will have the basis of a good routine for the baby and feel confident and calm as a mum. I know from experience that if you feel relatively organised within the first six weeks with feeding, bathing, dressing the baby, wrapping and nappy changes, you will be less anxious, more confident and enjoy your early parenting days. I want this book to be a positive guide for you in these first weeks as a parent. I want to be the positive voice in your head.

So many women tell me 'no one told me it would be this hard'. Maybe some people did tell you, but it's really hard to imagine that life until the baby arrives. Pregnant women tend to focus so much on labour and birth, and think breastfeeding and parenting will be easy and come naturally.

Labour is for one day but parenting is for life! Katy and Hughie, new parents who arrived home with their first baby, looked at each other and said, 'Is this legal that we are parents and know nothing about babies?' It's such a common feeling. You don't know what you don't know!

Let me tell you my chicken curry story. If we all decided to make chicken curry using the same recipe, we would all go out and buy the same ingredients, follow the recipe and in the end have more or less the same chicken curry.

This book is not a recipe book. You do not have to sit and learn, page by page, how to care for your baby. Your parenting must come from your heart. Babies aren't chicken curry, and every child is different. So is everyone's parenting style.

The child you have given birth to is his own person—some babies are active and noisy, some need lots of holding and cuddling, others just eat and sleep. It's not luck if your baby sleeps and bad luck or your fault if your baby doesn't sleep—that is who your baby is. But you can encourage him to sleep well by following my bath, bottle and bed routine (see page 129).

Your life experiences, professional advice and advice you receive from friends, society, social media, different trends and books can influence how you parent your baby. How you and your partner were parented also matters, so it's a good idea to discuss your approaches during the pregnancy— and try to come to an agreement on areas where you may potentially disagree.

When your baby is born he is a primitive, unaffected newborn. A blank canvas. He doesn't have conscious aware-ness of where he is or what he's doing and relies on you totally. He is unable to be angry, annoyed, resentful or cross with you. As parents we project our values and feelings onto a baby's physical reactions. Often parents think a baby who is crying when he has his nappy changed is 'angry' or 'distressed'. He cannot think or lie, he cannot understand what time of the day it is or be consciously aware of his actions. The reality is that he is likely feeling insecure as he is being undressed, and his primitive reflexes make him cry to make his parents aware he would rather have his clothes on.

I always tell new mums and dads there are things to worry about and things that are not worth the worry, energy and anxiety. All a well baby needs is food, love, warmth, security and cleanliness.

Things you should worry about

Be concerned and go to the doctor or a hospital if your baby:

- is floppy or unresponsive
- has jerky movements
- is a blue or dusky colour
- has a high temperature, over 38.5°C
- is not feeding well
- has constant or projectile vomiting
- is not having a lot of wet nappies
- has blood in his poo
- is crying uncontrollably and you cannot stop or settle him
- is coughing consistently.

Things you shouldn't worry about

- burping
- wind
- wet nappies
- pooey nappies
- a small amount of vomit
- hiccups
- an alert baby, looking around and not crying.

Fear in parenting

New parents receive a lot of fear-based information during pregnancy, childbirth and early parenting from professionals, Google and girlfriends.

Now, imagine if you are a new parent and you hear some or all of the following:

- Don't pick your baby up—he will get used to you holding him and he will never sleep by himself.
- Don't breastfeed your baby to sleep—he will never be able to go to sleep himself.
- Don't give your baby formula as it will stop your breast milk.
- Don't wrap your baby when he feeds as he will be too comfortable and go to sleep.
- Don't give your baby cow's milk, as he may have an allergic reaction.
- You must breastfeed or he will not get your antibodies.
- Don't breastfeed too long.
- Don't go straight to your baby when he is crying—he needs to learn to put himself to sleep.
- Put your baby down in his cot. Don't hold him too much, he will get used to it.

What all these 'don'ts' and 'must nots' do is instil *fear*. And fear can lead to insecurity and shame. As Professor Brené

Brown has said: 'Shame is an epidemic and to get out from underneath it, to find our way back to each other we have to find out how it affects us and how it affects our parenting. The way we look at each other—we have to understand our way back to empathy because empathy's the antidote to shame.'

So, like building a house, and to counter the fear, start by establishing basic foundations and routines from the day you arrive home from hospital.

Many 'baby routine' phrases are thrown at parents from books and community campaigns, but the practice—the reality—is always different from the theory. When new parents arrive home from hospital with a new and sleepy baby, they assume this is the way the baby will be. Within days or weeks, the sleepy baby wakes up, changes behaviour, is more alert, and sleep routines change.

Then what?

Everyone's tired, no one's getting any sleep or enough rest, and the family can be stretched to breaking point. It wasn't until I had my son that I realised how debilitating it is to be sleep-deprived every day and every night. He had reflux and 22 years ago there was no medicine to treat it, so it was a very long first eight months, feeding and holding a baby who was in so much discomfort. It's hard to parent 24 hours a day on three to four hours' sleep. It's incredible how you manage, but somehow you do.

I keep going back to the basics: food, love and warmth.

Feed your baby, wrap your baby, hold your baby, keep him close. These are the keys of early parenting and attachment. Be practical. You will not spoil your child if you love your baby and hold him close.

We are all overwhelmed when we become a mum for the first time. Don't overthink the newborn stage and don't read thousands of books or you will end up confused or anxious, or both.

This is your child. Trust your instincts and do it your way. Trust and have confidence in your natural ability to love your baby and yourself. Mother Nature has made not only our bodies very cleverly but our babies too—everything babies do, every movement, noise, reaction, they do for a reason.

You and your partner will love your baby the most in this world, and you will need to guide and teach him. It's up to you. Go with your gut feeling, with what you feel is right and always, always protect your child. You are, and will be forever, the voice in your child's head.

It is very difficult to comprehend the journey of parenthood no matter what anyone tells you. What is hard to explain is how hard this journey actually is, and that it is not like what you see in the movies. The beginning of this journey was hard, and at times quite dark, until Cath came in and turned the lights on.

As soon as you have a baby, everyone seems to have an opinion about everything. Even if you were confident before, you soon start questioning yourself because everyone seems to have their own way of raising a baby and they push their ways onto you.

The most important thing I learnt was to shut out all the voices, all the noise. From the moment I made the conscious decision to only listen to Cath, everything became easier. Because, as Cath says, it's not that hard! Everyone complicates things so much. Cath's was the only voice I heard and within the first few months my beautiful boy was sleeping through the whole night, I continued to breastfeed, and life became beautiful and simple.

Breastfeeding was very difficult, and so many times I thought I couldn't do this. With one visit or a phone call, I not only felt like I *could* do this, I actually did. Cath teaches more than just skills; she gives you the nurturing, love, compassion and a strength that only a passionate mother can give to another.

LINA

2

Getting ready

Having a baby is emotional and overwhelming. Just for a start, your pregnant body is completely different to your non-pregnant body. You may have lived all your life with no headaches, no constipation, no heartburn, no sinus discomfort, no waking every two hours to pass urine, no sleeping with twenty pillows to make yourself comfortable, no sore hips, no sore back and then, when you are pregnant, you may have all of the above—in one day.

Your body changes to accommodate your pregnancy and to prepare you for childbirth and lactation. You change physically and emotionally, regardless of whether the outcome of the birth is a vaginal birth or a caesarean section.

No one can really prepare you to have a baby—the physical changes to your body, the birth, the sight and smell of your newborn and the emotional highs and lows. And that's just in the first hour! For many women it's a major change to mind, body and soul.

The most important advice before the birth

Listen to your doctor and midwife. All other 'helpful' information can become overwhelming, confusing and only increase your anxiety. You need at least one constant and positive person in your life who will not confuse you.

I once had a first-time pregnant mum arrive at my rooms crying and very distressed. She told me, 'The dry-cleaner said my baby was too big.'

Her baby was overdue and the woman was feeling so vulnerable that the dry-cleaner's comment just tipped her over the edge. She cried all day. I'm sure the dry-cleaner had good intentions and is very good at her job, but she has never worked in obstetrics.

So, keep it simple, keep googling to a minimum and don't set yourself up for anxiety and needless worrying by comparing your pregnancy and your newborn to your girlfriend's or sister's. All babies are different.

There can be elation, excitement and joy but also doubt and uncertainty and at times more difficult emotions like fear, irritability, frustration and even anger. Emotions arise without us asking for them, and emerge from more primitive areas of the brain, beneath conscious awareness. While emotions of all sorts can be completely normal, trouble arises when we get caught up in strong emotions and are not able to think clearly and respond wisely.

Getting stressed is not our fault. Stress is a powerful mind–body response that has been hardwired in the human brain over centuries. The stress response can be traced back to times when on a daily basis there were very real threats to safety in the external environment. This hardwiring within our brains is such that when faced with threat, we were programmed to run away from danger as quickly as we could, and to ask questions later. When the threat response is activated it profoundly affects brain function, effectively disconnecting information processing from the sophisticated capacities of the frontal lobes which give us the capacity for creativity, lateral thinking and intuition—the very skills we need when we are faced with a distressed baby or partner.

DR DIANA KOREVAAR

Things to buy

Buying clothes and furniture for your new baby can set you back a lot of money if you want it to, but not all the gadgets and toys are necessary.

One of the most important things you will need is a strong pram. There are hundreds to choose from, so shop around and get one that is the right height for you so you can walk comfortably with it. Ensure there's enough room for baby accessories such as bags and clothes, and that you are comfortable with getting the pram in and out of the car. Believe me, you'll do a lot of that.

Always ensure that the pram conforms to the Australian safety accreditation, and there are strong safety straps so the baby is safely and securely fastened in at all times. And say goodbye to leaving the house with just one bag and your keys!

It's vital to have a professionally fitted baby capsule that is safe, strong and sturdy. You will need the baby capsule to bring the baby home from the hospital, so be ready and:

- have a qualified professional insert the capsule into your vehicle
- make sure you read all the instructions when you buy the baby capsule
- if you have friends with a baby take time to watch them put the baby in and take him out of the capsule
- don't leave it until the morning you are leaving the hospital to read the instructions.

Before the baby arrives it's important to get the house organised. Another essential item is a cot. The cot should be approved by the Australian safety standards so you can put your baby in the cot from day one if you choose not to use a bassinet.

You'll be doing a lot of nappy-changing, so make sure a change table or change area is at the right height for you and that everything is on hand—nappies, clothes, lotions and potions.

Never leave a baby alone on a change table, bed or couch. Even though a newborn cannot developmentally roll, he might move and squirm enough to fall off in less than a minute. I receive calls from distressed parents saying their baby has fallen from the change table, bed or couch. If you need to leave the room, place the baby either in the cot or on a rug on the floor. We were taught from day one that *if your eyes are off the baby, keep your hands on the baby*. Start from day one and this will become normal practice and prevent the baby from falling.

A comfortable chair is a good idea in the nursery so that the mother or whoever is feeding the baby is comfortable and relaxed.

I encourage you to buy an electric steriliser, some bottles and some formula before you go into hospital. Using microwave sterilisers and boiling water when you're tired and distracted can cause accidents. There are many excellent brands around; I consider it $150 well spent.

With bottles, it doesn't matter what type of bottle you get since the baby just wants to suck. What I do suggest is that the teats be on the longer side and thick, rather than short and round.

There is an abundance of baby monitors around these days. Not everyone wants or needs a monitor and many people have the baby with them in their room for the first six to twelve months. Again, that is up to you. Most monitors come not only with voice and movement recognition but also a video so you can observe the baby sleeping.

It amazes me that there are so many different baths you can buy for a baby when all you really need is a large and uncomplicated bath. Please don't look at a bath with a seat in it because floating in warm bathwater is one of the most pleasurable sensations for your newborn baby. Sitting a baby in the bath is not necessary and when you hold the baby correctly in a bath without a seat the baby will float and relax. Bathing the baby is one of the nicest times for both him and the parent, and should be one of the safest.

Everybody loves a new baby, and you will receive gifts and many clothes from generous friends and relatives when the baby is born. Beware of well-meaning friends who drop off bags and bags of old clothes. Sometimes it's their way of clearing out old baby clothes and dumping them on you. Be upfront about what you do and do not want.

It's important to buy some wraps for the baby. I recommend light muslin wraps, about 1.2 metres in length and 1.4 metres in diameter (see 'Cath's Wrap' on page 138). You need up to ten wraps and at least ten singlets and ten changes of clothes. When a baby has a big bowel action you will be surprised by not only how loud it is but also how much there is, so have plenty of changes of clothes handy, and especially in your nappy bag, as it always happens when you are out and potentially unprepared!

If you intend to breastfeed make sure that you are fitted professionally for a bra. Your breasts enlarge within the first sixteen weeks of pregnancy and again after you give birth, so you need to make sure the bra will completely cover your full breasts when your milk comes in, usually between days three and five after the birth.

I see so many women with very small lacy bras with full, bulging, engorged breasts and they look so uncomfortable. It's really not the time to be looking sexy! Most big department stores employ trained professional bra-fitters in their lingerie sections. Bring the bras into hospital with you and wear them from day one. You can wear underwire bras during your pregnancy but not when breastfeeding as the underwire can press into your full and sensitive breast, causing damage to the breast tissue.

Most hospitals will give you a list of baby clothes to take to the hospital, depending on the season. There is a general list for you to follow on page 18.

And please don't put any mittens on the baby. Babies instinctively put their hands to their mouths, which means they can chomp on the mitten and pull it off, making it a potential choking hazard.

What to take to hospital

It's best to have your case packed and ready to go by about 34 weeks, earlier if you wish. On page 18 is a general list for a new mum staying in hospital for four to five days. If you are having twins or triplets you will need to double or triple the baby clothes.

One last checklist

This covers some of the practical things you will need to organise before the baby arrives. What follows is by no means comprehensive, just the important basics.

- If you are having your second or subsequent baby, organise childcare with family or friends. Keep their phone number on the fridge.
- Put your blood group card and GBS status in your packed suitcase. Group B streptococcus, a type of bacteria found in the vaginas of 20 per cent of women, only affects those babies born vaginally. You will have a vaginal swab at 36 weeks to check if the bacteria is present. If the test is positive, you'll be given antibiotics during labour and the baby will be given them after birth.
- Pack your case (including baby's clothes) by 34 weeks.
- Once finished, put the case in the boot of the car so it's ready for the big day.

What you'll need in hospital

The mother
- Stretch pants in dark blue or black (4 pairs)
- Comfortable T-shirt tops that you can breastfeed in
- Underpants: buy black underpants
- Well-fitted bras (3)
- Nursing pads for leaking breasts
- Maternity pads (3 packets)
- Comfortable shoes/slippers
- Pyjamas for overnight feeding
- Toiletries

The baby
- Onesies (7)
- Singlets (7)
- Muslin wraps (7)
- Hats (2)
- Clothes for going home
- Soft nail file for baby's nails
- Disposable nappies and wipes if the hospital doesn't supply them
- Formula and bottles, supplied by all hospitals

Incidentals
- Blood group card
- Any correspondence from your doctor, e.g. GBS status
- Change of clothes for your partner
- Chargers and/or batteries for phones, laptops, cameras
- Plastic bags for dirty washing to be taken home

- Put some old towels and large plastic rubbish bags in the car. If there's a chance your waters may break, put the plastic bag on the car seat and the towels over the plastic. Amniotic fluid is not compatible with leather car seats! Also place a pad and a towel between your legs, as there can be a few ongoing gushes of fluid.
- Unpack the steriliser and learn how to use it. A simple gadget is hard to put together when you are both sleep-deprived.
- Learn all about the baby capsule and how to strap a baby in. Have it safely installed by an authorised facility.
- Keep the car full of petrol—sounds basic, but you'd be surprised how many cars run out of petrol on the way to hospital!
- If your partner is staying with you in the hospital, redirect your mail and newspapers or have a neighbour collect them for you.
- Have a plan/carer for your pets.

3

Happy birthday

All women labour differently. Most women would prefer a vaginal delivery but at the same time we all want a healthy outcome for mother and baby. I've seen countless babies born and just as many different reactions from the mothers. I can still remember this wonderful, nameless, faceless midwife standing behind me who said, when our son was about to be born, 'You are going to be a mother in two minutes.' It was fabulous to hear and is still in my head today, 22 years later.

The day you have your baby is one of the most wondrous, exciting days of your life, even though you might feel simply exhausted and overwhelmed after you have given birth.

Hospitals and birth centres

In my 40 years of working in labour wards in hospitals and birth centres, and witnessing one home birth, I have seen a lot of changes in the postnatal care of women. In the 1970s women stayed in hospital for ten to fourteen days after they had their baby. To many mothers today that seems excessive and I suppose it was, but we got to know the mums really well, there was a continuity of care and fabulous education programs within hospitals and, as midwives, we certainly saw new mothers through the early challenges of a new baby.

As a young midwife I saw how the mother's body would change in the days after the baby was born. We were patient as we waited for the mother's milk to come in and did not hurry them to lactate by expressing the breasts on day one to get 1 ml of colostrum and feed it to the baby with a syringe. We very rarely used a pump or expressed mothers with well babies. Usually we only used a pump, and only did so if the baby was sick or premature. We spent time with women, sitting with them and teaching them how to attach the baby properly, guiding and supporting them.

> So much happens in that first six weeks. I'll just say that
> I still have your handwritten copy of how to set out my
> day and night carefully stored in the filing cabinet. Salt
> baths, get ready for bed yourself first so you can collapse
> once baby's down, bathing baby later at night so you only
> have to get up once . . . all that good stuff. I used it for
> Amy and I'll be using it again!
>
> NIKKY

Home births

A home birth is important for some parents, but that area is beyond the scope of this book. In the spirit of full disclosure, I am not comfortable recommending home births, a position I have developed after having attended the birth of more than 10,000 babies. During this period, there have been a number of births where being able to access the services and skills of a hospital at very short notice was key to the health and survival of the mother and/or the baby. Complications, unfortunately, still happen in childbirth. Fortunately, they are uncommon. But for those women and babies who experience unexpected complications, it's crucial that they have immediate access to the right specialists and resources.

Not all birth experiences are the same. My recommendation is that parents-to-be focus on finding the doctors, midwives and hospitals they feel compatible with and who they feel they can best work with. If home birth is the direction you want to go in, you should get advice from people who specialise in this area.

Childbirth and pain relief

I have seen amazing progress in pregnancy, childbirth, care of the newborn baby and postnatal care over the past 40 years. Thankfully we do things better and have better outcomes for both mothers and babies. While there is more intervention, the outcome has been more healthy mothers and babies.

If our grandparents had had access to the medical assistance and intervention we now have in 2016, I know what they would have chosen. I'm sure our grandmothers would not have chosen to have their babies at home; they would have had ultrasounds during pregnancy to check on the health and growth of the baby, and they would have embraced foetal monitoring if required during late pregnancy and labour to ensure a healthy baby in utero and for early diagnosis of foetal distress in labour.

If it meant the life of either the mother or child were assured, they would have had elective caesarean sections to ensure a live, healthy baby, and they would have been induced into labour. I'm sure they would have loved the idea of an epidural that posed a low risk to the mother and no effect on the baby, plus a pain-free and shorter labour.

Up until the mid-1970s heroin was used as pain relief for women. It sounds frightening, but heroin worked especially well for first-time mums having a long labour. The problem was that after they gave birth they really didn't have much memory of the labour, plus the side-effects on the mother and especially the baby were enormous. There were not too many other options then.

When heroin was removed from hospitals, in came the narcotic analgesic pethidine, which is still given today to women in labour. Pethidine is very strong and does have a direct effect on the baby. Pethidine is an extremely appropriate drug for pain relief *other* than when given to women in childbirth.

If asked, most women who had pethidine during labour say it made them feel sick, it wasn't effective and often the baby was not interested and alert for breastfeeding after birth. Women are not told about this, and pethidine is nearly always offered to women during labour.

Only two things will take away the pain of labour. One is to have an epidural, and the other is to have the baby! These days women are educated in what to eat and what not to eat—no alcohol, no soft cheese and so on—but our system is still readily offering a strong narcotic analgesic such as pethidine that has a direct effect on the baby! It has never made sense to me.

Since epidurals have come into use for women in labour, Australia now has a rate of 50 to 60 per cent epidural use in private hospitals for women having their first baby, and 35 to 40 per cent in the public system. In the 1980s the downside of the epidural was that they were so effective the woman had no sensation and the outcome of her labour meant a definite episiotomy and forceps delivery of the baby. This was very traumatic for new mums. Over the past ten years the progress in epidurals has been amazing. There are anaesthetists who are highly trained in giving epidurals to women in labour.

I have come full circle regarding my attitude to pain relief in labour. In the early 1980s I was in charge of one of Melbourne's birth centres where women came to give birth without any pain relief, supported by me and the other midwives. I was committed to this practice, as I was concerned about the way women were given narcotic analgesics with little to no choice of either an active or drug-free childbirth. I supported many women over a number of years to achieve a natural and drug-free childbirth.

Today, I encourage the use of epidurals if the woman wants one as they have no effect on the baby and women feel in control and clear-headed to participate in labour and the birth. Not only do they give adequate pain relief and shorten the length of labour, women recover quicker from the birth experience. For a woman labouring, the epidural can allow her to have enough sensation to push the baby out and, at times, without tearing or an episiotomy.

Reasons for having an epidural

- takes the pain of labour and childbirth away
- safe
- no effect on the baby
- women dilate quicker due to the use of oxytocin to augment labour
- women feel more in control in labour and when giving birth

- less traumatic
- women recover faster physically.

Myths about epidurals

- increases the risk of a caesarean section. **No**
- has a direct effect on the baby. **No**
- lengthens the labour. **No**

Side-effects of an epidural

- headache
- sore back
- infection
- failure of procedure
- nerve damage.

Partner support during labour

Most partners are really excited about the birth of the baby but I'm sure there's deep underlying anxiety about watching their loved one go through pain and discomfort and having no control in this situation. This is normal: even medical people who become fathers for the first time and who are very comfortable within a labour ward or an operating theatre feel anxious when their partner goes through labour and birth. Who goes into the labour ward is up to the mother-to-be, and also depends on hospital policy.

In a labour ward the midwives will explain and advise the partner on what is happening and how the labour is progressing. Some helpful things for the partner to do while the woman is labouring are:

- hold her hand
- reassure her she is doing a great job
- offer a sip of water after each contraction
- place a cold face washer on her brow or behind her neck if she finds it comforting
- make sure you eat and drink enough
- if you feel dizzy or a bit nauseated, sit down and tell the midwives.

It is really amazing to watch the birth of your baby. Even though many say they are not going to look at the actual birth, by the time the baby is born, most partners feel comfortable enough within the birthing room to watch.

A newborn baby doesn't look like babies in the movies—those 'newborns' are usually six months old and smeared with strawberry jam. Babies who are just born are usually a bluish/whitish colour, often with some blood, mucus and vernix (the waxy white cream coating the skin of newborn human babies) covering them.

Some babies cry as soon as they are born, and some babies need a little tactile stimulation to start them crying, but that first cry is the most beautiful sound you will ever hear. (And then, for the next months, you will try to stop him crying!)

Babies who are distressed at birth will need assistance to breathe, and all staff are fully trained to assist a baby in distress.

Most doctors will offer you the chance to cut the umbilical cord—or, as I say, 'declare the baby open'. If you have any anxieties about that, the midwives and doctor can help you.

Nearing full term, our little girl flipped into the feet-first breech position. Thankfully modern medicine meant I could deliver safely, but the timing was slightly devastating. Rob, my other half, was contracted to work in America, leaving one week before her birth. It was then that Cath joined forces with my mother and became my 'birth husband', a name we still fondly use for her.

Needless to say I was in an unknown world, this being my first child, and in my delirium I believe I even asked Cath if she had delivered a baby before. She laughed and took it with good grace, as she does with everything, and proceeded to hold my hand all the way to the finale.

On the day of the birth, she defied all the rules and filmed the arrival of our baby girl so that minutes later, on top of a mountain in New Mexico, USA, Rob was able to watch his daughter come into the world, on an iPad.

He didn't miss a moment. Cath's handholding continued well after that day. The support and advice she gave was immeasurable.

She is ever present in our life. I will always remember her . . . and her red lipstick and smiling face.

AYISHA

Cath shot the best film I have ever seen; I can never thank her enough for what she did for us.

ROB

Spreading the good news

These days one SMS can send the news of the baby's birth around the world within seconds. It's good to have a list organised on your phone so you only need to send one SMS. Your phone will go into meltdown once you send the message, so be mindful of when you send your good news. You will get hundreds of responses—everyone loves the happy news of a new baby being born. Don't be in too much of a hurry: enjoy some precious family time, just the three of you.

Ten things to do in the first hour after birth

- Look at your baby's beautiful face.
- Maintain skin-to-skin contact (keep a warm blanket over him to keep him warm as he may be wet and his temperature can drop quickly).
- Smell him: it's amazing how beautiful newborns smell.
- Count his fingers and toes.
- Have one of the midwives take a photo of you, your partner and the baby soon after birth.
- Kiss him.
- Say hello and tell him who you are.
- Look at your partner; it's one special moment.
- Check his genitals—even if you knew what you were having it's good to check!
- Enjoy every minute.

After birth

So, congratulations! You did it. You have a baby. It's amazing and life-changing. It's overwhelming, exhausting, miraculous and confronting. Some women shake, shiver, feel nauseated and may vomit straight after birth as the body reacts, and although you are madly in love with your baby, often it's matched by a feeling of exhaustion and relief.

For the first few hours after birth the baby is sometimes alert and looking around. This is the time to examine your baby to see that he has all his fingers and toes, and to gaze at the beautiful face you've been waiting to see. Some babies have a lot of mucus in their mouth and throat after they are born, particularly babies born by caesarean section. When babies are 'mucousy' they may gag and/or vomit up the mucus. Hold your baby upright if this happens, and if you are concerned about him, call one of the midwives to check him immediately.

The baby is injected with vitamin K at birth, and the immunisation program begins with a hepatitis B injection. The midwife looking after you will discuss these injections with you both before the birth.

In 1952, American obstetric anaesthesiologist Dr Virginia Apgar developed a scoring system to assess the effects of obstetric anaesthesia on babies, and it is still used at every birth today. The Apgar score is used to assess the condition of the newborn at birth on five simple criteria, on a scale from zero to two, which sums up the five values. A healthy baby at birth would gain 9/10 for his Apgar score (a point is usually not given for the bluish colour of the baby at birth). On the next page is an example of the Apgar score chart.

After the excitement of birth has settled down, and the doctors and midwives are happy with you and the baby's condition, the birth room is suddenly quiet and empty, with

Apgar sign	2	1	0
Appearance (skin colour)	Normal colour all over (hands and feet are pink)	Normal colour (but hands and feet are bluish)	Bluish-gray or pale all over
Pulse (heart rate)	Normal (above 100 beats per minute)	Below 100 beats per minute	Absent (no pulse)
Grimace ('reflex irritability')	Pulls away, sneezes, coughs or cries with stimulation	Facial movement only (grimace) with stimulation	Absent (no response to stimulation)
Activity (muscle tone)	Active, spontaneous movement	Arms and legs flexed with little movement	No movement, 'floppy' tone
Respiration (breathing rate and effort)	Normal rate and effort, good cry	Slow or irregular breathing, weak cry	Absent (no breathing)

only the three of you there, and you start thinking, *What just happened?* It really is an unreal and exhilarating feeling.

The first few hours can give the new mother a false sense of security. You think, *I've got the best baby who's just going to feed and sleep.* Just wait until week two, when we talk about the wakeful and noisy baby!

The physical reflexes the baby has when naked after birth belong to a group of primitive reflexes. The Moro or startle reflex is when the baby's hands reach out to try and grab hold of either the mother or somebody else to keep them feeling secure. Remember the baby has only felt security in the uterus—when he moved, the uterine wall buffered his movements. So that is why I encourage you to wrap your baby for all feeds and all sleep for up to six months. (See page 138 for 'Cath's Wrap', which maintains your baby's security during feeding and sleeping.)

Your blood loss after the birth will be heavy, more than a first-day period, but will slow down over the next six weeks as the uterus involutes (the process by which the uterus returns to its pre-pregnancy size, shape and position within your pelvis). Blood loss will slowly lighten in volume and darken in colour. If at any time you notice an offensive smell in your vaginal blood or experience a very heavy flow—I mean pouring down your legs—you need to seek medical advice.

As you breastfeed your hormones are released, so when the baby sucks the nipple it not only lets down your milk but also stimulates your uterus to contract and involute. You may feel a gush of blood in the early weeks along with some period cramps during and after breastfeeding. As the blood pools in your vagina you will pass the pooled blood (blood clots) either when you go to the toilet or onto your pad when you stand up and move around. The uterus is back in the pre-pregnant position six weeks after birth, ready for another pregnancy—no pressure!

Women having their second and subsequent babies may find these afterbirth pains extremely painful and require strong pain relief. (Some women say the afterbirth pains are equal to or worse than labour pains!)

Tight and expensive shorts do not help your uterus go back into shape faster—it's your brain and hormones that naturally help your body. I see so many women feeling really uncomfortable wearing tight shorts straight after birth. The shorts are fine when you have healed and are feeling more comfortable. Give your body a good three to four weeks to heal, trust your body—then wear the shorts. Mother Nature has it all organised.

At this time you think you will never have sex again, let alone another baby, but the perineum is a very forgiving area and heals very well. Give your body a good six to eight weeks of physical recovery. And you will have sex again!

Recovery after birth

Once you have settled in the labour ward, the doctor and midwives are happy with your blood loss, and the epidural (if you had one) has worn off, you will be transferred to a postnatal room after you have had a shower. This is where you will rest and recover, learn how to feed your baby, wrap him, hold him, change his nappy, bath him and all the other skills that you will need to get through the next few weeks.

The day after the birth, you may feel like you have limitless energy and are full of beans. But you've just had a baby and your body needs to recover. Even after a straightforward vaginal birth you will have a tender vaginal area. Don't be afraid to ask for pain relief. There are no prizes for putting up with pain.

After a vaginal birth with an episiotomy (plus or minus haemorrhoids) you will feel really very sore, and four- to six-hourly medication will be offered. The introduction of anti-inflammatory medications as pain relief for postnatal pain has helped women with after-birth pains, episiotomy pain and full, sore, engorged breasts.

After a caesarean section you will have a sore abdominal area and be given strong pain medication. The first day post-caesarean, you are really very sore and you need to rest. You need to recover from the birth of your baby as it is major abdominal surgery. Keep ahead of your pain and do not play catch-up with medication because pain is debilitating.

You're sleep-deprived, you've got a baby to feed, you have a sore bottom or abdomen and a lot of visitors to talk to—all of this is very tiring. Pain relief won't affect your baby, but it will help you. Don't worry about the medication potentially making you constipated. I always tell new mums to take pain relief, as it's best to be out of pain. We can always treat and manage constipation.

Please do not look at your perineum (the area where an episiotomy is performed). I have received many distressed phone calls from women (and their partners) thinking they are in all sorts of trouble because the perineum is swollen, bruised and stitches are evident—as often the stitches fall out as they heal. If you are in pain that is not resolved by oral medication, please seek medical advice rather than getting out the mirror for a look.

As medical professionals we know how a perineum recovers and heals, what it looks like in the stages of recovery. Even though we know how sore it is, there is a process of healing that must take place before you will be comfortable again. Like any wound, the body begins healing immediately but it takes time. Think of a bad bruise on your leg and how very sore it is on day one, then it changes colour and is still swollen on day two. As the days go by the wound feels worse before it feels better. A caesarean section wound and an episiotomy are no exceptions. Be patient with your body's healing process, take your pain relief, have a salt bath daily—add a handful of table salt to your bath—and if you have any concerns contact your doctor or the hospital where you gave birth.

After you pass urine or open your bowels, wash yourself down with warm tap water (use a plastic bottle or jug), then pat yourself dry with a clean towel and put on a new pad. Ice packs, along with consistent pain relief, help with swelling in the early days.

Due to recovering from an emergency C-section and having problems breastfeeding, the first six weeks were fairly bleak for me. I thought it would all come so naturally, that I would know exactly what to do, but the reality was much different to what I had spent the previous ten months imagining.

I quickly learnt to not be so hard on myself, to read my baby's cues, to trust myself and not constantly act on the advice from everyone around me. But most importantly I learnt that the happiness of my baby was the most important thing, and that it was OK if my grand parenting plans needed to change to make that happen—for example, making the switch from breastfeeding to formula-feeding.

KATE

The first feed

The most important feed for you and your baby is the first feed after you have given birth. It's important because you have waited so long to have your baby in your arms and your baby is ready to suck. If your baby is well, healthy and born at term, he is usually alert, crying and ready to suck vigorously at the breast. The baby will suck for the next couple of hours after the birth and then sleep for quite some time. This is very safe if your baby is well, at term and a good weight. The baby is still hydrated with the amniotic fluid he has been drinking in utero. Even though the baby is sucking for quite some time he will not get a huge amount of volume from the colostrum, but it is really rich in kilojoules (calories). Colostrum also works as an initial laxative for the baby so he may pass his meconium (his first poo) within hours of birth—the first nappy change for you.

It's really important to wrap the baby after birth to keep him warm and feeling safe and secure. There is plenty of time for skin-to-skin contact, and if the baby is left unwrapped, his temperature can drop. Keep your baby wrapped when feeding and then let him sleep.

Sleepy baby

Most babies are sleepy for around the first few days after birth while you are in hospital. There are a few causes: one is just the natural hibernation that a baby goes through a few hours after birth. Midwives encourage new mums to give the well, healthy, full-term baby a really good breastfeed in those first few hours that they are awake and alert after birth because we know that the baby will then sleep for quite some time. (If the baby is premature, sick or in the special care nursery this approach does not apply.)

The well baby

When babies are born at term they are physically examined by the doctor, midwives and, in some cases, a paediatrician. A paediatrician is always present at a caesarean section to care for the baby. A well baby has good colour, has good tone in his muscles, sucks well at the breast, passes wee and poo frequently, cries when undressed and when his nappy is changed, and after a good feed will sleep soundly either in his cot or in your arms.

If you are ever concerned about your baby's health, seek medical advice quickly. The best option for a baby less than six weeks old is the closest hospital that has doctors with expertise in neonates and young babies.

The newborn baby check

The newborn examination, much like any physical examination of a patient, is designed to screen for and detect any obvious physical abnormalities that may exist. Up to 10 per cent of all infants are born with anything from minor to major physical abnormalities.

Below is a checklist that the paediatrician would routinely follow for any baby, usually within the first two days after birth, or before if there is a need to check the baby. It is thorough and it's important for you to understand what the paediatrician is doing. As medical professionals we see so many well babies that we can usually identify those who are unwell very quickly. Anything that seems abnormal in a baby is observed, diagnosed and explained to you.

Your MCH nurse will also examine the baby again at the first and subsequent visits. The check may take the practitioner fifteen minutes to finalise. Here is the list of what the doctor will be checking and why.

First, the doctor will ask you about your birth, as it's important for him to know if there have been any difficulties or issues at or after the birth. The doctor will also ask about your method of feeding (breast, formula or mixed) and if:

- the baby has had any breathing difficulties
- the baby needed any resuscitation or help with breathing at birth

- there are any congenital issues that run in the family, e.g. heart
- there are any issues with hips in the family
- your baby has passed his first bowel action (meconium)
- your baby has passed urine.

The doctor will then take off the baby's clothes, leaving the nappy on until he is ready to check the genitals.

My friend and colleague, paediatrician Dr Brendan Chan, explains the newborn check. The list below details the major systems/areas that are examined, and a number of aspects that are checked. It is not designed to be an exhaustive list.

- **Head** Does the shape look normal? Are the suture lines (gaps separating the bony plates of the skull) present? Are the anterior and posterior (front and back) fontanelles, the soft spots on the baby's head, open?
- **Face** Do the face and facial features look normal? Is there a cleft lip or cleft palate?
- **Eyes** Is the red reflex ('red eye') present? An abnormal red reflex may indicate a congenital eye abnormality such as a cataract.
- **Upper limbs** Are there five fingers on each hand? Do the arms look normal? Is the collarbone broken? (It can be if there is shoulder dystocia—difficulty in delivering the shoulders in a vaginal birth.)

- **Lungs** Is there any increase in effort of breathing, when listening with the stethoscope to the breathing in both lungs? Breathing difficulties are common in the newborn period, often due to infection, prematurity of the lungs or retained fluid in the lungs, known as transient tachypnea of the neonate.

- **Heart** Listening to the heart sounds with the stethoscope, are there any heart murmurs, which may indicate a congenital heart problem?

- **Abdomen** Are there any abnormal masses? Sometimes organs such as the liver and spleen may be larger than normal, or there may be unusual growths in the abdomen.

- **Hips** Are they stable? Are there any clicks on movement? Does the leg dislocate out of the hip socket? This check is for a congenital condition called hip dysplasia.

- **Genitalia** Do they look normally developed? In a boy, are both testicles present? (For a boy, there can be differences in the way that the shaft of the penis and foreskin form— hypospadias. The testicles may be undescended.)

- **Anus** Is the anus present? There are rare occasions when the anus does not form.

- **Lower limbs** Are there five toes on each foot? Do the joints and rest of the legs look normal? There might be abnormal-ities of bone development or development of the digits.

- **Back** Are there any dimples in the lower back? These may indicate a form of spina bifida.

- **Muscle tone** Is there strength of muscle tone in the arms, legs and core? Does the baby move all limbs equally? If not, this may indicate a neurological or nerve power problem.

Ten things you may not know about a newborn

- They can shudder as if they are cold (they also do this while in utero).
- Sometimes their eyes roll around when they're asleep.
- They breathe irregularly.
- They purse their lips.
- If they vomit, sometimes it also comes out of their nose.
- They may vomit and gag on mucus after the birth.
- They have hair on their ears and back.
- They have swollen and enlarged genitals.
- They are very noisy overnight.
- Female babies can have a mucus and blood discharge from their vagina.

Babies born unwell or prematurely

Not all rules apply to all babies in the first four to six days. There are premature babies, babies of diabetic mothers, little babies, very hungry babies, babies with congenital abnormalities, babies with breathing difficulties and jaundiced babies. All these babies are treated differently.

Premature babies are placed in a special care nursery. Some are too tired and too little to even suck, so they are given a supplementary feeding formula plus the mother's breast milk through a little tube called a gavage tube, inserted via their nose into the stomach. The baby can then be fed while he sleeps and grows and becomes strong enough to suck at the breast or the bottle.

These babies start with sucking one bottle a day, plus six to eight tube feeds, progressing to more bottles and fewer tube feeds, to more breastfeeds and fewer bottle feeds. It's all done slowly and methodically under the paediatrician's direction and the midwives' care in the special care nursery. (See page 94 for expressing breast milk for premature babies.)

If they have low blood sugar, the babies of diabetic mothers may require formula within an hour or two of birth. A blood test done by a heel prick can predict the blood sugar level (BSL) of the baby. If it is low the paediatrician may request the baby have a breastfeed, formula-feed or, if the BSL is very low, an intravenous drip (IV) of sugar and water to stabilise him. During his life in utero he has been ingesting a high level of sugar but when he is born his sugar level falls dramatically, so he may need treatment to bring his sugar levels up.

Babies who are born at term but are little (under 2.5 kilograms) are often hungry and need not only breast milk but also additional formula to help them gain weight quickly. These babies have often had a placenta that has been working a little slower than normal and that's why they are smaller than the average baby.

The hungry baby needs food, either breast milk or formula or both. There is absolutely no use in trying to express 1–2 mls of colostrum from the mother, causing her discomfort and anxiety, when she has a screaming baby at the breast. The colostrum is not going to go away. If the baby is hungry and crying and not attaching to the breast, the sensible way to settle the baby is to give him some formula. You only need to give him a small amount and he will feel less hungry and more settled. Then, after a sleep, he will attach to the breast and feed more effectively. It's simple, easy and makes sense.

A baby with breathing difficulties will require care by a team of paediatricians and midwives in the special care nursery until his breathing is stable.

Jaundice

Not every baby becomes jaundiced. Babies in utero have a high concentration of red blood cells. When born the baby's body breaks down the blood cells that it doesn't need and some of the red blood cells end up staining the skin, causing jaundice. The liver is the last organ to wake up after a baby is born, and since that is where red blood cells are metabolised, that is why babies get jaundice. Some babies have 'breast milk jaundice', which is caused by an enzyme in breast milk. Some jaundice can take a few weeks to fully leave the skin.

If the baby is jaundiced a blood test, called a serum bilirubin (SBR), will be done in the hospital to check the level of jaundice in the blood. If it is over the safe level the baby may be put under ultraviolet lights, which break down the blood cells in the skin. Jaundice causes sleepiness in babies, which means they don't feed very well. You may need to express your breast milk and give it to your baby via a bottle or give him some formula to maintain hydration. Once the jaundice has resolved and the baby is waking up you can reattach him and continue breastfeeding.

A low-weight baby at term

If you have a low-weight baby, the only thing you have to do is feed, feed, feed.

I have set out below how I propose feeding a low-weight baby who is around 37 to 38 weeks' gestation and around 2.5 kilograms. If you push a low-weight baby to suck at the breast too early he will get too tired and lose weight. By giving him expressed breast milk and formula he will gain weight and strength, and the mother will breastfeed for longer during the first year.

- Try to express five times a day, ending the last express at 10 pm, then sleep overnight and wake and do the first express for the day at 5 am.
- Feed the baby every three hours day and night with expressed breast milk and/or formula.
- To conserve the baby's energy, don't bath him until he weighs 3 kilograms.
- Once the baby weighs 3 kilograms and is eager to suck at the breast, offer him both breasts for ten minutes on each. Don't express that feed.
- Gradually increase the breastfeeds as the baby grows stronger and is capable of sucking at the breast, and decrease the expressing.
- Continue to give one bottle of formula after the bath each night.
- Feed on demand as the baby needs.

Tongue-tie

Tongue-tie or ankyloglossia is a congenitally thick lingual frenulum under the tongue, resulting in reduced mobility of the tongue. Around 5 per cent of babies have mild tongue-tie. It is common for some paediatricians, midwives and lactation consultants to encourage new parents to have the tie snipped in the early days after a baby is born. A trained professional snips the frenulum under the tongue with a pair of sterile scissors.

Personally I find the snipping of tongue-tie invasive, painful and unnecessary. I have consulted with experienced obstetricians; ear, nose and throat surgeons; oral and maxillofacial surgeons and dentists about this, and they all agree that it is a totally unnecessary and invasive procedure for newborn babies. Some professionals tell new parents that tongue-tie is to blame for their baby not sucking, for sore nipples and for potential speech problems when the child is older. This puts the fear of God into the new mums.

If I were an uninformed new parent and a professional told me that the tongue-tie is causing my sore nipples, and that it will affect my baby's sucking and lead to potential speech difficulties, I suspect I would have my son's tongue-tie cut too—at one to three days of age. In severe cases, where the tongue is split at the tip of the tongue, nothing need be done until the child is old enough, when an experienced specialist surgeon will operate under a general anaesthetic. The maturity of the tongue as the baby grows is a factor against having the tongue-tie cut.

Be patient and let nature take its course. Wait. It is not an urgent situation, and if you have issues with the baby attaching, please use nipple shields first (see page 77 for more information). A nipple shield helps a baby with tongue-tie breastfeed as it adds length to the nipple and enables the baby to suck. All babies with tongue-tie can feed properly when being fed by a bottle, as the teat is long, so they will feed well off the mum if she has a nipple shield on to help the baby attach. In my practice I have never encouraged any parent to have their baby's tongue-tie cut, and I have never had a baby I couldn't assist to attach to the breast and suck.

Why you should delay snipping the tie

Let an oral and maxillofacial surgeon carry out proper excision of a tongue-tie around ten years of age when the lower anterior teeth have preferably erupted. Snipping of the tongue-tie soon after birth is not recommended for the following reasons:

- Possible damage to the ducts of the submandibular salivary gland may result from early surgery.
- Merely excising the tissue under the tongue does not solve the problem as there is also tissue attached to the alveolar ridge, which should be removed.
- Allowing for growth of the mandible, especially laterally, will allow the tongue to increase in size and reduce the need for surgery.

MR JOHN CURTIN

Your noisy, healthy baby

Your baby will make lots of different noises and can be very, very loud. This can be disconcerting at first, because you don't know what he means. All the noisy snorts, squirming, choking sounds, coughs and grunts are quite normal, but it can be very difficult for adults to sleep at night.

It does settle down in a few weeks but babies with gastric reflux (see page 165 for information on gastric reflux) are particularly noisy at night. They grunt, squirm and even sound like they are choking on their milk, which causes so much concern and anxiety to new parents. I often have parents video their baby to show me how they are sleeping and grunting, squirming and making all sorts of noises, as they think it's so abnormal for such a little baby to make such a racket. It's reassuring for the parents to know this is normal. If, however, the baby turns blue or dusky at any time, seek medical advice.

Sometimes, after a big feed, your baby may get the hiccups. This is due to the baby having brought up wind, and is a normal body process. Half of all the calls I receive in my practice are about wind. New parents are often concerned about their baby having wind or not burping. If it doesn't come up (as a burp), it will come out (as wind/gas).

All babies have wind. We all have wind. It's a normal body process and it's not life threatening. I would be concerned if a baby didn't have wind. When your baby is well, he will drink, he will hiccup and he will burp and maybe pass wind all at the same time. Don't worry about the little things that the body does normally and naturally. His tummy will gurgle and he will pass wind.

When I was pregnant, many people would ask if the baby was going to sleep in my room, usually followed by a smug grin and the statement 'babies are very noisy'. I imagined a few sniffles, maybe even a little cute grunt or two, but thought, *How much noise can a tiny baby really make?*

The smug grin was justified! As first-time parents, my husband and I were not prepared for the terrifying and concerning noises a baby makes, especially one with reflux. Our daughter's reflux started when she was around ten days old and it made sleeping for us nearly impossible. We would attempt to lie her down in her bassinet at night, but within a few minutes the noises would start.

My husband described the sounds she made as a 'drowning with pneumonia'. To provide some symptomatic relief from the reflux we were advised to raise the head of her bassinet (along with medication), but still the gasping, gagging, squeaking, gurgling, choking and snuffling noises continued. You could not believe that a tiny baby girl could produce such alarming sounds. Even white noise—noises that replicate the 'whooshing' sound in utero—would not take the edge off the alarming sounds emerging from the bassinet. For weeks on end the only way our baby would sleep without these frightening noises was sitting upright in our arms.

The sounds, which resulted from gastric reflux, were really terrifying and it was difficult not to put your adult equivalent lens over the noise and diagnose that we may have a very sick baby. As new parents we found it very distressing to hear and had to be constantly reassured our baby was not sick and this was 'just' reflux. Nine weeks down the track our baby Chloe is so much better and not as noisy!

JESS AND CHARLIE

Baby's belly button

When your baby is born, your partner is given the chance to 'declare the baby open' by cutting the umbilical cord. Once the cord is cut and trimmed down by the nursing staff you need to take care of the cord stump. Many years ago we used antiseptics to keep the cord clean and the cord stayed on longer, became very smelly and at times infected. Now we just use water and let the body's natural healing process take over; the stump separates in around five to seven days. It is safe to bath the baby at all times when the stump of the cord is still attached.

As the belly button starts to dry out over the next few days it will heal and be like any normal scab. As it separates from the skin you may find there's a little blood on the baby's singlet. Don't be alarmed, it's perfectly normal and only happens because of the separation of the scab from the skin. Ensure that the belly button is clean and dry at all times.

If the belly button becomes smelly or there is a red area on the surrounding skin, please consult your doctor. It will take at least a week for the belly button to be clean and for the stump to fall off.

Partners and support

When I first started midwifery we learnt about 'the minor complications of pregnancy'. I would think to myself, having heartburn, constipation, haemorrhoids, varicose veins, nausea, vomiting, headaches, mild muscle cramps, insomnia and frequency of urine all together were hardly 'minor'.

While most partners are as excited about the baby as the mothers, they do not go through any of the hormonal changes that a woman's body goes through. I have had many women tell me their partner does not understand how they feel, which is absolutely correct. Often the partner is a voice of reason, as he or she has not changed hormonally.

I would encourage all new fathers to be as hands on as they can be. Attend appointments with your wife. Read a few books. Ask questions and take as much of the mystery out of it as you can. I found that by doing so, I felt surprisingly ready when our baby son arrived. It allowed me to enjoy the experience and be involved, certainly a bystander no longer.

JULIAN

The hospital sleepover

It's really up to you if you would like your partner to stay in hospital with you. Some partners prefer to go home and sleep in their own bed; others stay full time. (Arrangements can be made in some hospitals for partners to sleep in the room with the new mother and baby.) If it's your second or subsequent baby your partner may like to go home to be with the other child or children. Some go to work while their partners are in hospital and take leave when their partner and baby come home. You should work out what works best for you.

While you're in hospital it is time to recover, feed your baby and seek assistance and guidance from the midwives about the care of your baby. They are there to provide education and assistance.

Conflicting advice in hospital

Unfortunately, you'll receive a lot of conflicting information in hospital about breastfeeding and the care of your baby. You might have fifteen midwives looking after you over four or five days and, trust me, you will have as many different opinions given to you! This is very bewildering for new parents, who often leave the hospital more confused than when they went in.

As a new mother, trust your basic instincts and your love for your baby. Your baby knows what to do and so do you! He doesn't need to learn how to suck, he knows how to suck, as it's a primitive reflex, and Mother Nature has hardwired him to live and not starve.

Because of medication during and after the birth you will need to make sure you have a good poo by at least day two or day three. If you are in hospital the midwives will ask you each day and if there is no success they will give you something to help you along—they will want you to open your bowels before you go home. If you are home and haven't opened your bowels, take a gentle laxative.

You won't rip or tear when passing your first motion. It's often the anxiety that makes you worry, but you will feel so much better when that is ticked off the list. If you continue to take pain relief when you go home, ensure you have a good bowel motion every day. Eat lots of fruit and vegetables and drink 1–2 litres of water a day.

Controlling visitors

A new baby brings so much happiness, and relatives and friends want to share in your joy and excitement, but some-times it's a little too much too soon. Visitors can be very, very tiring. Prepare yourself before you've had the baby. Organise the people you would like to come and see you. Funnily enough, many people don't want to see you—they just want to see the baby.

Years ago, hospitals had a nursery where all the babies were on show, but now we have the baby in with the mother and the room can be filled with not only flowers but also too many visitors, leaving the mother and baby stressed and upset.

For the first day it's really great to see your parents, siblings and grandparents. Good friends will come in and say hi, look at your beautiful baby, say what a good job you've done and leave. Friends, neighbours, school friends, the grocer and random visitors really need to wait. Most hospitals have a sleep time where mothers and babies are not to be disturbed.

Ensure your family and close friends are up-to-date with their immunisations. We currently have an epidemic of whooping cough, and newborn babies are susceptible.

After the visitors leave I've seen so many women just sit and cry, completely overwhelmed. Often the new mum has a sore tummy or bottom, plus hot throbbing breasts and is really in no mood to discuss the birth for the umpteenth time. Your partner can manage the crowds visiting you in hospital. They can SMS friends and acquaintances saying no visitors for a few days, or no visitors until you are home and settled. Ask the hospital staff to limit your visitors before visiting hours or, if you feel confident enough, say to your visitors, 'The baby needs a feed, so thank you for coming. Do you mind leaving?' The hospital staff can also do that on your behalf.

Some patients inform people before they have the baby not to visit at all. It's up to you but at least have a plan.

When my wife was pregnant, I would think of the many things I didn't know about caring for a child. I didn't know how to change a nappy, I didn't know how to swaddle an infant, I didn't know how to bath and clothe a newborn. Those were things that I knew that I didn't know and would have to learn.

DAVID

Going home

Leaving the hospital and taking your baby home is an incredible feeling. You've got the baby capsule ready and all of a sudden you think, *Oh my goodness, there are so many drivers on the road*. You did not realise how fast people drive until you are taking your new family home. Everything has changed now that you have your precious baby in the car!

When I left hospital as a new mother I can remember thinking, *I'm taking this baby home*. I had previously waved goodbye to so many new families, and now here I was, bringing my own son home. Back then, we used to carry the baby down to the car and wave goodbye to the new family—a lovely tradition.

Driving your new family home

Here are some tips for making that first car trip with your baby a safe and happy one.

- Ensure you have enough petrol. Don't laugh—I have seen quite a few people run out of petrol and believe me, the new mother is never impressed.
- Make sure the boot is empty and there is enough room to bring home the case, baby gifts and flowers.
- Arrive at the hospital early, as discharge is usually around 9 am.
- Ensure the baby capsule is correctly fitted.
- Park close to the hospital and put the parking ticket in your wallet.
- Have some change/cash.
- Pack the car and, once you have finalised the paperwork with the discharge office, strap your baby into the baby capsule.
- Drive home safely!

4

The first few days ...
and into the first week

Babies are like flowers: when they are born they are all closed up and quiet, and as the weeks go by they open up, wake up and look around, and gaze at the world.

A baby can have 'visual fixation' shortly after birth. Their visual acuity during the first few days—the ability to distinguish details and shapes of objects—is a bit like a camera that is out of focus and blurry.

Within a week of birth a baby can focus on objects about 20 centimetres from his face, so keep your baby close and smile, talk and get to know him, and tell him how much you love him. This should become your natural talk to him, and your voice will be in his head forever, knowing that he is loved. He needs to know your face, as you are going to stick around for quite some time.

The sleepy baby wakes

Babies can get their days and nights around the wrong way for the first couple of weeks, and it can be very demanding to have a nice calm baby during the day who just feeds and sleeps, but who wants to party at night, and no matter how much you feed him, wakes up ten minutes after you put him back to bed.

I believe the baby gets his days and nights mixed up in the first few weeks because he has been rocked in utero by his active mother during the day and when she goes to bed at night to rest, he usually wakes up and stretches. This becomes the only 'routine' he knows, so when he is born it takes about two weeks for him to get the days and nights in the correct order. Women who have had a baby will recognise this pattern—you are so tired when you are at the end of your pregnancy and when you finally go to bed the baby seems to wake up and dance!

Be patient—everything takes time to settle down with a newborn. The baby will wake up and, while you feel like you are in the eye of the storm that is sleep deprivation, you will get through it, the baby will feed during the day, and you will all sleep. I know you will get through it, but when you are in the midst of it the nights seem long and lonely. It takes time and patience and a whole lot of love to get through these early days with the newborn baby. My bath, bottle and bed (BBB) routine, which we will go into at length on page 129, really helps with this process of changing the newborn baby's routine.

The pattern is usually something like this: your baby is sleepy initially for the first 48 hours, after which he wakes up and you feel you cannot fill him up. Day two post-birth is often a long night, especially if it's your first baby and in the past few days he has been quiet and peaceful. He is starting to lose weight and is hungry. He feeds and cries, feeds and cries, and you keep getting conflicting advice on how to manage this wakeful and noisy baby. If you feel you are constantly feeding and your nipples are tender or grazed, there is only one thing 'wrong' with the baby—he is hungry and awake.

This is the time you consistently feed and feed and feed and your nipples become very sore. If he continues to demand and you are so sore, offer him a small top-up of formula. You do not need to express any milk—you have had him on the breast and the formula is some well-needed 'free calories' that the baby needs.

Your brain does not know you have given him formula, so nothing will happen to your lactation. It is a given after you have had a baby and doesn't just disappear. As women we are hardwired to lactate after we have given birth. As soon as the placenta is expelled after the baby is born the brain knows that it has to 'feed' the baby. That is why women in Africa, for example, who are often low in nutrition can still breastfeed their babies since lactation is a brain function.

In some hospitals you need to sign a consent form to give your baby formula. I find it completely insulting that new parents have to give permission for their babies to be given food! It's hard enough if you have a baby crying, let alone having to sign a 'consent form' to give your baby food that is made for babies, leaving you feeling guilty.

Babies need food

Some babies are born little, some babies are born big, but all babies are hungry. They need to be fed. You cannot overfeed a baby but you can underfeed a baby. I've seen far too many babies who have been underfed and diagnosed with colic, reflux and allergies, with professionals telling their mothers they have 'an incorrect latch'.

In many cases they just needed some extra food—and that food is milk and not 1–2 mls of colostrum. Some babies need 20–30 mls of formula to satisfy their hunger. Often new parents are told that their baby's stomach is only the size of a marble, which it is. Its scares parents to think they will 'overfeed the baby and the stomach will burst', something I've been told by many patients.

What is not explained to new parents is that yes, the stomach is small, but it empties into about 7 metres of small bowel. We need to teach new parents in simple terminology so they will understand their baby, and not fear what they might do to them. As Einstein once said, 'If you can't explain it simply, you don't understand it well enough.'

Back in the days when women stayed in hospital for ten to fourteen days, midwives understood and trusted the process of how women's bodies changed as the milk slowly came in over days three, four and five. The babies were sleepy and were offered formula overnight so the mothers could rest and recover from the birth. We never let babies scream with hunger, and we made sure they were fed as we waited for the mother's milk to come in. These babies rarely lost 10 per cent of their birth weight as they do now and they were not screaming with hunger. We would sit with the new mums for hours, teaching them about breastfeeding, and we didn't rush them out of hospital.

I know the economies of scale have changed over the years and a hospital stay is very expensive, but this care can be continued at home. For some women it is actually better to go home within 24 hours than to stay in hospital for four days. In my opinion, the fourth or fifth day is the worst day to go home as, for some women, their milk hasn't come in or their breasts are full and engorged and/or the baby is waking up, so they go home feeling confused, perhaps not feeding successfully and anxious.

Midwives are extremely well trained and have really good intentions but unfortunately they only see women postnatally for the three to four days while they are in hospital. Their advice is correct for *those* few days, but not applicable as the baby grows, wakes up, and changes his feeding and sleeping patterns. And believe me, a baby who is one, two, three or four days old is a very different baby from one who is one, two or three weeks old.

What new parents do is refer back to what they learnt in hospital from the hospital midwives and that's how they continue to care for the baby. I see it time and again with the mothers I care for.

Take, for example, the sleepy baby, a very common sight in the postnatal ward in the first few days. Many midwives encourage parents to undress the babies and unwrap them, to keep them cold, flick them on the toes, blow in their face, put a cold face washer on the body to wake the baby up so he is uncomfortable and will suck properly. I still cannot believe anyone teaches parents to do that.

Mother Nature does not want babies to be cold. To me it is ludicrous that anyone would tell a new parent to undress their baby and make them cold and uncomfortable so they feed. It just doesn't make sense, and when I explain the alternative to parents they all say to me it never 'felt right' to them either but they did as they were told. When you are a new parent on your own in hospital you're vulnerable, and when you have a professional telling you to undress your baby, blow in his face and flick his feet, you do it.

New parents are the easiest and most compliant of all patients to care for because they want to do the right thing for the baby, even if their gut feelings say otherwise. I made a home visit to a new mum whose baby was three weeks old. She called me to say that her baby would not stop crying and she was at the end of her tether. When I arrived (it was in the Melbourne winter) her baby was just in her nappy and singlet and she was screaming! I asked the mother why she undressed the baby to feed her. She said that was how she was taught in hospital.

The mother is a very intelligent woman who held a high and responsible position before having a baby. I explained to her why she may want to dress the baby, and wrap her to feed her and keep her warm. When we did that, the baby fed on both breasts and went to sleep. The mother said she had never seen her do that. There were lots of tears, shame, sadness and frustration. She told me she knew what was right, but had to believe what she had been told in hospital. The baby continued to feed well after being dressed and wrapped, and the mother continued to breastfeed for twelve months.

Breastfeeding

According to the World Health Organization (WHO):

Breastfeeding is an unequalled way of providing ideal food for the healthy growth and development of infants;

it is also an integral part of the reproductive process with important implications for the health of mothers. Review of evidence has shown that, on a population basis, exclusive breastfeeding for 6 months is the optimal way of feeding infants. Thereafter infants should receive complementary foods with continued breastfeeding up to two years of age or beyond.

Breast milk is the best food for a newborn and growing baby. If you get a good and supported start, breastfeeding is such a wonderful experience for both mother and baby.

Over my 40 years of working with mothers and babies I've supported and encouraged every woman who wants to breastfeed. No two women lactate in the same way, and the information given to women prenatally makes them feel that breastfeeding is easy. It isn't: to breastfeed successfully you need a lot of support, education and patience.

Breastfeeding doesn't just happen for every woman; milk does not simply come in on day four and that's it. And there is no need to give women such a hard time if they don't want to breastfeed or are not successful with breastfeeding. Every woman is different, so don't feel guilty if you can't or don't want to breastfeed your baby. At your child's 21st birthday party no one will be discussing whether he was breastfed or not.

While exclusive breastfeeding is ideal, not all women can or want to do so. I know that introducing a bottle of formula early does prevent exclusive breastfeeding, but I know my patients breastfeed for longer—that is, up to and over twelve months.

As you can see from the statistics below, we are good at starting breastfeeding—that is, mothers have good intentions to breastfeed—but if the ongoing support is not there I know women will give up and formula-feed their baby. The information our new mothers are receiving from hospitals and within the community is leading to a sudden drop in breastfeeding once the parents are home with the new baby.

In 2010–11 a national infant feeding survey was conducted by the Australian Institute of Health and Welfare, which found that:

- around 96 per cent of breastfeeding was initiated for children 0–2 years of age
- at four months of age, 69 per cent of babies were still receiving some breast milk, but only 39 per cent of babies were *exclusively* breastfed up to three months of age
- at six months, 60 per cent of babies were still receiving some breast milk, but only 15 per cent of babies were exclusively breastfed to five months.

During the late 1970s and 1980s I was so passionate about women breastfeeding exclusively that I was referred to as a 'radical and militant breastfeeding midwife'. I have changed over time; I learnt that this generation wants their partner to be more involved and give the baby a bottle. Some mums feel so guilty and experience a sense of failure as a mother if they cannot or don't want to breastfeed. There are times when women want to give in and stop, but with the correct support, encouragement and care, the hurdles that seem huge to the new mum can be overcome. When the mothers are tired, sore, sleep-deprived and don't feel as if they are successful with breastfeeding, often it is their support system of family and friends or the voice in their head that says give up.

Breastfeeding takes at least six weeks to establish and for the mother–baby connection to develop. The most important days to get yourself into a rhythm with breastfeeding are the first seven days of the baby's life. If you get this right, can hold the baby in a way that's comfortable for you and the baby, and even relax while you breastfeed, you're part way there. As long as the baby is attached to the breast and sucking, your milk will come in—be patient and try not to get obsessed with expressing.

I spoke to a new mum who has a three-month-old baby. She said, at the end of our call, 'I want to thank you for your support during those first six weeks. I was so ready to give up but so glad I didn't. I am now exclusively breastfeeding and the baby is sleeping all night.'

But not everyone can or wants to breastfeed. Women who have previously had breast surgery, such as for breast reduction or implants, do not lactate as well. Their milk will come in and they can feed initially, only to find they don't have enough breast milk for the growing baby. I advise women who have had breast surgery not to expect to exclusively breastfeed. In my experience they definitely need to top up the baby with formula after every breastfeed, especially for the first six to ten weeks. Initially they will be able to satisfy the baby with their breast milk but as the baby's needs increase they will need some formula. Doing so means they will also breastfeed for longer, as they will not have a hungry baby.

If you have 100 women in a room, each woman will lactate differently; in fact, each breast may lactate differently. One woman I know successfully breastfed her three babies on one breast only. Personally I breastfed my son for a long time, it worked well and I was so happy to be able to continue to feed even while working out of home—and I never expressed once.

Lots of mothers worry they won't make any milk. Remember that lactation is a given. Your body knows it needs to lactate. When your baby is born, the placenta is delivered and your brain knows to trigger the body to make milk to feed the baby. When the baby sucks, oxytocin is released from the mother's brain and enters the bloodstream, causing ejection of milk from the milk ducts. This is what's called the letdown reflex.

As the baby starts sucking you will feel the letdown reflex occur but in every woman the sensation is different. Some women feel nothing; others feel a tingling in the nipples.

Some women feel pain in the breast, others feel a dragging, pulling sensation in the breast. Some women even feel it under their arms and in their shoulder. Whatever you feel, that is your body working well to let the milk down for your baby.

WHO and UNICEF recommend new mothers:

- initiate breastfeeding within the first hour of life
- breastfeed exclusively—that is, the infant only receives breast milk without any additional food or drink, not even water
- breastfeed on demand—that is, as often as the child wants, day and night
- do not use bottles, teats or pacifiers.

Some women do achieve all of the above but in my experience this is not sustainable for everyone for a variety of reasons, including insufficient breast milk to sustain a hungry baby, the use of bottles for complementary feeds, and parents choosing to use dummies.

In practice and in my experience, today's generation of mums can find it difficult to exclusively breastfeed and feel guilty if they can't, mummy-bashed if they don't, and ashamed if they won't. The mums I look after use one bottle of formula after the bath routine at night, which does not affect their lactation, and I can confidently say they tend to breastfeed for longer, which is a fabulous win/win for both mother and baby.

The sucking reflex

Your breasts have been ready for lactation since you were sixteen weeks pregnant. Let your baby suck when he is awake and let your milk come in gently. Too many midwives start expressing women by hand or by a pump in the first days when it's so important not to touch the breast and to let the baby suck. From the baby's first breastfeed your brain will have the message to make milk when the baby is sucking. There is no hurry as your milk coming in is a given.

Babies want to live. They want to suck to get milk and sustain life. So make it easy for yourself and put *your* baby to your breast rather than have the midwives do it for you. You need to find your voice and say that you are happy to have a go at feeding your baby.

Keep your baby close, hold your baby in your arm (left arm if feeding on the left side) and let the baby attach himself to the nipple—he will suck at the nipple. He will do it himself, he doesn't need to be shoved on or be held by the back of his head or shoulder by a midwife. *You* can do it. He is very clever and innately knows how to open his mouth, take the nipple into his mouth and suck. If your baby is sucking, he is attached to the nipple—it's that simple! You don't need to have the entire areola (the dark area around the nipple) in your baby's mouth. For some women that is virtually impossible as their areolas are so large. The nipple changes during pregnancy, darkening and enlarging the areola. Just remember, if the baby is sucking, he is on!

Sucking is a baby's strongest reflex. I explain to new mums that your new baby cannot talk or walk yet and his strongest reflexes are to suck and cry so he can live. He will cry to alert you to his needs, and his suck is strong and vigorous, as that is the only way he can grow and live. A new baby's primitive instincts are to find the nipple and suck and suck and suck until he is satisfied. Trust your baby.

Attaching a baby to the breast has become quite a clinical, complicated process in hospital. I believe if we leave mother and baby together and let them work it out, we can have successful attachment. There are too many rules and regulations about holding and positioning the baby, talking to the baby and telling the baby to open its mouth. Your baby doesn't know what day it is, let alone understand you telling him to open his mouth!

Babies start to suck their fingers, fists, hands or thumbs in utero and continue to put their fingers to their mouth for quite a few months after birth. It's not uncommon to see a 'sucking blister' on the hand of a baby who has been sucking away while growing and enjoying life inside the uterus. This innate hand-to-mouth reflex is normal and one reason why we should not put mittens on a baby's hands or cover his hands with the ends of his growsuit sleeves. Mittens can be dangerous too: if he puts his covered hands to his mouth he can pull the mittens off, causing a choking risk.

Every mother and her baby are individuals, and I make sure that what I do is working for that particular mother and her baby. Some women have an abundance of milk, which makes it easier for the baby to feed well, gain weight and sleep; others have less milk, or the milk comes in slowly and the babies need extra kilojoules (calories) besides breast milk.

Also, everyone has different nipples. It is easier if they are nice long nipples for the babies to attach to and suck since how well the baby will suck is all about nipple length. If the nipple is not long enough or the baby is unable to attach due to flat or inverted nipples, a nipple shield is perfect as it adds length to the nipple and allows the baby to attach and suck. Nipple shields can be the difference between breastfeeding and not breastfeeding (see page 77).

Twenty-point guide for successful breastfeeding

1. Wrap your baby for ALL feeds. Wrapping your baby's hands gently is most important. It is not advisable to wrap your baby's hips and legs tightly, as the hips need to be in a constant 'frog position' for growth and development. See 'Cath's Wrap' on page 138.

2. If you have a well baby, do not express any milk—let your baby do the work. He is the best pump!

3. Hold the baby across your chest with his ear in the crook of your elbow, on his side facing you. If you are feeding from the left breast, place him in your left arm.

4. Let him suck the nipple in by himself, rolling him into your breast with the arm that is holding him. Do not force him on by hand or let anyone else hold his head and force him onto your breast. Your baby has an innate, primitive will to suck and live, and to live he must suck your milk.

5. It's black and white—if your baby is sucking your nipple he is ON the breast and sucking well! Don't keep taking your baby on and off the breast, as this will damage your nipple.

6. Hold your breast with your right hand with the peace sign. Three fingers below the nipple, one above, very gently pressing your breast to help your nipple face upwards so the baby's mouth can find it.

7. You do not need to get all the areola in. Some women have large areolas and it is impossible for the baby to have all this in his mouth.

8. If your baby has not passed urine and is losing weight, give him some formula as free kilojoules (calories). This will prevent weight loss and a crying and distressed baby,

and you and your baby will feel better and your breasts will continue to fill.

9. DO NOT massage your breasts or lumps at any time. Your breasts are inflamed and working very hard. Compare your lactating breasts to a swollen ankle: you would not massage it as it would cause harm (and pain) to the tissue—the same applies to your breasts. Don't touch them and don't let anyone else massage them.

10. Use anti-inflammatory drugs and paracetamol for sore breasts.

11. Put only breast milk on your nipples. Do not use any creams, potions or lotions on your nipples. This can lead to infection and mastitis.

12. If your breasts are hard, swollen and red, apply cabbage leaves that have been washed, dried and stored in the freezer. Flower them around your breast (avoid the nipple) and remove when they are warm and soft, then reapply more cold cabbage leaves. Wear a well-fitted bra or a firm singlet.

13. If there is not enough milk coming out of your engorged breasts, leave them and feed your baby formula while you wait for your breasts to settle. Do not express or pump your breasts.

14. If your breasts are engorged and have flattened your nipples, use a nipple shield to add length to your flattened nipples. When your breasts have settled the baby will attach to your nipple again to suck.

15. If you have flat or inverted nipples, use a nipple shield. They are the difference between you breastfeeding and not breastfeeding. They are soft and easy for the baby to attach to.

16. If you have damaged, sore and/or cracked nipples, DO NOT take the baby off the breast. Put on a nipple shield and your nipples will be healed within 24–48 hours. The wonderful healing power of the breast milk pooling within the shield will heal your nipple quickly.

17. Feed your baby frequently. Never use water or sugar and water, just breast milk and/or formula for babies younger than twelve months.

18. If your baby is still hungry, give him some formula. He will gain weight faster and you will breastfeed for longer.

19. You cannot overfeed a baby.

20. Do not give a hungry baby a dummy. The dummy has no kilojoules (calories) and the baby needs food—milk.

Nipples and nipple shields

I've seen thousands and thousands of nipples! Some nipples are long and the baby can attach easily and feed well. Some are not so big. Some are inverted with the pointy part of the nipple going back into the breast. To breastfeed successfully your nipple needs to be sucked by the baby to the back of the baby's tongue, which stimulates the baby to suck and then swallow, suck then swallow.

There is help available if you don't have long nipples and can't attach the baby to your breast, or if you have grazed, cracked and sore nipples. When I first started midwifery, nipple shields were thick, hard and not pliable, and I very rarely used them. These days nipple shields are fabulous. They are soft silicon shields that fit over the nipple and not only provide protection to the sore nipple but also add length to women who have flat, inverted or little nipples. The breast milk pools around the cracked nipple and heals it quickly.

When I produce nipple shields for women who have been having problems attaching the baby to the breast or who have sore and cracked nipples, the new parents both look at me in amazement and wonder why they haven't been offered them before.

Most shields come in a standard or medium size (I wouldn't get a small nipple shield). Even if you think your nipples are tiny it is better to have a bigger shield than a smaller one.

Women with flat or inverted nipples can successfully breastfeed a baby using a nipple shield. If the nipple is flat or inverted the baby cannot draw the nipple deep enough into its mouth, therefore causing damage to the tip of the nipple, cracking and a lot of pain. The baby also tends to fuss a lot at the breast if the nipples are flat or inverted, as he cannot satisfactorily attach and suck at the nipple.

I have seen a lot of women with flat or inverted nipples use nipple shields and successfully breastfeed. Then, usually at around twelve to fourteen weeks, the nipple has been properly drawn out through constant sucking and the baby is able to attach directly.

Don't feel guilty if you have to use a nipple shield. Believe me, they help and always make the difference between breastfeeding and not breastfeeding.

For some reason, some midwives and lactation consultants attach a fear factor to nipple shields. The alternative to a nipple shield is to express or pump, and to give the baby the milk in a bottle or even a cup. This takes time and energy, and causes a lot of anxiety in the new mother.

My baby was seven days old. My nipples looked like they were going to fall off. There was no way I could put the baby to the breast—her suck was so strong and I was in so much pain. Cath wrapped her and showed me some nipple shields and away we went. The feeding was 80 per cent instantly better once I had the nipple shield on and continued to improve. I cannot believe how quickly my nipples healed and I continued to breastfeed. If you are in pain and your nipples are sore, grab some shields and give them a try. They were the only reason I could continue to breastfed.

CLARE

Nipple pain

Some women experience severe pain while breastfeeding, while others feel no pain at all. One of the most distressing is the needle-like pain that shoots up the nipple through the breast. I have seen women who have the pain shoot up through their neck, shoulder and even down their leg! The pain can happen during feeding and also continue between feeds. For some women it gets so bad even the thought of breastfeeding their baby becomes stressful, and the new mum nearly resists feeding as they don't want to go through the pain again.

For some women expressing decreases this pain. This is an alternative so the baby can still have breast milk, but it is not sustainable. If the pain continues after the feed there is a simple way of decreasing the pain. I ask the mother to place her open hand over her breast with her nipple in the centre of the hand. I then ask her to flatten the breast with her hand (this needs to be done gently due to sore breasts and nipples). If the mum holds her hand firmly there for 50–60 seconds the pain will decrease and in some cases go away altogether. This needs to be done every time she feels the shooting pain.

In some cases it may be thrush, but not always. I treat the mother for thrush using oral anti-fungal tablets that can be bought over the counter at the pharmacy. I do not change the mother's diet in this situation.

Kate's story

Kate first saw me when she was sixteen weeks pregnant with her first baby. We talked about her desire to breastfeed but she told me that her nipples were both severely inverted. I checked her nipples at that time and really, I hadn't seen nipples that inverted in my 40 years of practice. I advised her that she would not be able to breastfeed without nipple shields.

I advised her to put nipple shields in her case so when she was in hospital she had them ready to use. The first few days after her baby was born she had soft breasts. The baby was able to attach, but there were a lot of problems, many hands and many different midwives. Kate contacted me on day three with very full breasts, very sore nipples and a crying, hungry baby.

We wrapped the baby and I reminded her about the nipple shields and showed her how to use them. The baby attached immediately and sucked one side then fell asleep. The nipple shield was full of Kate's breast milk and her breasts were soft and comfortable after the feed. We unwrapped the baby, changed her nappy, did a little bit of tummy time and rewrapped her and attached her to the other side using a nipple shield. I can remember Kate sitting there, feeling so proud that within 20 minutes she had fully breastfed her baby. She could see that she had enough milk, but most importantly, her baby was content and asleep.

Kate went on to breastfeed Sophia for about eighteen months. At four months her nipples had been drawn out well enough and the baby was alert, strong and eager enough that she just attached herself to the breast without a nipple shield. You may not always need to use a nipple shield while you feed; it all depends on you, your nipples and your baby.

Last year Kate was surprised to find that she was pregnant with twins. The twins were born premature and needed assistance with feeding via a gavage tube and then a bottle. Kate had a lot of breast milk and could nearly provide the babies with enough breast milk for the entire time in hospital. Due to their difference in weight and development, the babies—a boy and a girl—were at different stages of attaching to the breast. Again we used nipple shields and I can report that Kate successfully breastfed her twins.

Breast engorgement

And just when you think you are getting used to this breast-feeding caper, you might experience engorgement, where your breasts feel full, hard, heavy, tender, hot and swollen; sometimes you may even have a slight temperature. Only in a few women does breast engorgement happen, but when it does it's a shocker.

Engorgement of the lactating breasts is caused by the build-up of blood, lymphatic fluid and milk in the breast ducts, and even though you have a lot of milk the baby is just not up to taking it all away. The worst thing to do is to pump or express engorged breasts.

The good news is that engorgement means you have good lactation, and it usually settles down in a few days. The bad news is that it is extremely painful, and sometimes women who have breast tissue under the arms find it can become engorged and as sore as their breasts. Due to the breast fullness, the nipples also tend to flatten, and often babies who have been successfully attaching to the breast cannot attach to the flattened nipple. A nipple shield is perfect to use until the breasts have softened.

After the breast engorgement has settled down you may have a really good supply of breast milk. You always seem to be leaking or dripping milk, the baby only takes a little and is full, and when he starts to feed and you let down you feel like you're choking the child because he is coughing and spluttering due to the force of the letdown. If you have a lot of milk and the baby is only drinking a small amount and it's quite uncomfortable, rather than expressing your milk and causing a vicious cycle of soft breast and full breast, use a nipple shield. What the nipple shield does is slow the flow of the milk coming out, so the baby gets fewer squirts of milk.

Always feed the baby from both sides during the feed. The brain does not discriminate when it lets down the milk—both breasts have milk and you need to keep the milk moving to prevent mastitis. This may mean you only feed for a limited time on the first side, unwrap the baby, change his nappy and then rewrap and feed for however long the baby needs on the other side. When starting the next feed do the opposite—feed for a limited time on the breast you finished feeding on and then whatever the baby wants on the other side.

Mastitis

Mastitis is an infection in the breast that can occur during breastfeeding. It's usually an ascending infection, spreading from a crack in the nipple. It doesn't happen to everybody but for some women, unfortunately, it happens frequently.

Women with mastitis feel terribly ill and can become sick very quickly.

It is important to know the signs of mastitis so you can catch it early. Often the first signs are a headache and a sore throat along with a hot, red area on the breast that causes the mastitis. You can also experience flu-like symptoms such as hot and cold flushes, shivers, shakes and a feeling of general malaise. This feeling can take over within minutes and you feel very sick very quickly. As soon as you see a red mark on your breast, see your doctor. Try not to wait until you feel very sick.

You will need pain-relief tablets and anti-inflammatory tablets as well as antibiotics—all prescribed by your doctor. Never take anyone else's medication.

It's very hard when you have mastitis, because you still need to feed your baby. Even though you feel unwell and your breasts are sore, you need to keep breastfeeding because the milk needs to continue to flow. It's very important to have the baby suck on the breast that has mastitis.

Do not massage your breasts when you have mastitis. This is a common practice encouraged by some practitioners, but in my experience, massaging the breast actually makes things worse. Instead, put on a firm bra, take your medication and let the baby feed. Clean, cold (stored in the freezer) cabbage leaves flowered around your breast will provide tremendous relief (see also page 88).

Once you start antibiotic therapy you should start to feel better within 24 hours. If you don't feel any change, go to your doctor or local hospital straightaway as mastitis can form into an abscess and you can become extremely ill. Trust your body. If you don't feel well, tell somebody and get help.

Symptoms
- bad headache, often the initial sign
- sore throat
- aches and joint pains
- hot and cold rigors (sweating)
- red, sore patches on the skin of the breast.

Causes
- ascending infection from cracked and damaged nipples
- taking the baby on and off the breast too many times during feeding rather than letting the baby suck in the nipple to the back of his mouth
- full and engorged breasts
- massaging or rubbing breasts.

Treatment
- Take antibiotics: ensure they are the correct antibiotics, usually Flucloxacillin (make sure you are not allergic to penicillin before taking these).
- If the headache persists, take paracetamol or something stronger.

- Take anti-inflammatory drugs.
- Line your breasts with cabbage leaves.
- Always wear a firm, large bra with no underwire, or a firm singlet top.
- Keep the baby breastfeeding.
- Feed both sides even if it means limiting one side so your baby takes both breasts and keeps the milk moving.
- Only express if your baby is too sleepy and cannot attach.
- Use a nipple shield if your baby cannot attach because your breast is too full.

What not to do
- DO NOT massage your breasts or lumps: it can lead to a breast abscess. Think of your red, hot, swollen, inflamed breasts as broken ankles.
- Don't put hot packs on your breast.
- Tongue-tie does not cause mastitis.

Managing engorged breasts

- If your nipples have flattened and the baby cannot attach, please put a nipple shield on and feed the baby with the shield just until your breasts settle down. Using a shield will let you keep the baby on the breast rather than expressing and giving the baby a bottle, which is far too time-consuming.

- To feed the baby, take off your bra and top so it is easier to attach the baby when your breasts are so full. Often when the baby is sucking on one side the other side starts to leak, so put a hand towel over the opposite nipple to catch the dripping milk.

- Use medication such as an anti-inflammatory and paracetamol for pain relief and don't wait until you are in unbearable pain—keep ahead of your pain.

- The baby may only be able to suck a small amount at a time because of the volume of your milk. If this is the case feed five minutes on the first side, unwrap the baby, change his nappy, rewrap him and then attach him to the other side. Ensure the baby sucks both sides.

- **Do not** massage your breasts as this can cause terrible damage to your breast tissue.

- Even after a feed you may not feel that your breasts have softened. It is tempting to express to make them soft but once you start expressing your brain will just start responding and you'll be back to square one. Expressing is like taking one step forward and three steps back.

- Don't put any potions or lotions on your nipples—just use some breast milk that is either left on your nipple from the feed or is in the nipple shield.

- Wear a firm, well-fitted bra. This is not the time for sexy, lacy bras. Nursing bras are not the most attractive bras, but my goodness they are comfortable.
- Use cabbage leaves. For a 24- to 48-hour period you probably need at least four to six cabbages. Just clean one cabbage at a time. Fill the sink up with cold water, core the cabbage and separate all the leaves, washing them in the cold water. Dry them then place the leaves in the freezer and, when cold, remove and arrange them around your red, hot and throbbing breasts. There is no need to cover your nipple with the leaves. Put on a firm bra that completely covers your breasts or a firm singlet or T-shirt that makes you feel well supported and comfortable. When the cabbage leaf gets warm and soft, throw it away and put another frozen leaf on the breast. (After this process you will never want to eat cabbage again!)
- Rest when your breasts are engorged—you will feel quite emotional and often think that you are never ever going to be free of this pain. Be patient, your breasts will settle.
- Feed the baby as frequently as he needs, usually every two to three hours.
- Keep your fluid intake up, rest and eat.

- Within 72 hours you will still have full breasts and a lot of milk but the engorgement will have settled down and your breasts will have softened.
- If you have any redness on the breast, headache, sore throat and signs of mastitis, please contact your medical provider as soon as possible as you may be getting mastitis and will need antibiotics.

Not enough milk

Some women just don't make enough breast milk to sustain an adequate milk supply for their baby's consistent growth and development. If you do not have enough milk there really isn't much you can do, but do not stop breastfeeding. The best outcome is for you to breastfeed your baby and top him up with formula.

In my experience nothing can increase the amount of breast milk you have. If you pump or express, it just takes the milk out of your breasts, it doesn't make more. Expressing when you have a low supply tends to lead to obsessive pumping that is not physically or emotionally sustainable for you. I have spoken to and cared for so many women in the postnatal period but not one has said she enjoys expressing breast milk with a pump. Expressing isn't a normal part of breastfeeding, and it is only important if you have a sick or premature baby.

Just as you cannot change the colour of your eyes, you also cannot estimate how much or how well you will lactate. It's just the way *you* are and there is no tablet, medicinal concoction or herb that will increase your breast milk.

Women who don't have a lot of breast milk tend to feed and feed and feed the baby and often the baby is still crying after hours of sucking. It is *really* upsetting and an emotional situation for mothers, but my best advice is to give the baby as much breast milk as you can and top him up with some formula. I promise you will all be happy and the mother need not sit on a pump eight to ten times a day as some books and websites suggest, taking away precious time from her new baby.

If you breastfeed your baby and top him up with formula:

- your baby will be well fed and consistently gain weight
- you will be happier
- you will breastfeed longer
- your baby will sleep as he is well fed.

I promise you that a baby who sucks on the breast six to seven times a day with the formula top-up will not get confused or learn to refuse the breast. Mother Nature is too clever for that. But if he is not given a bottle early enough in life he will refuse it, and if you don't have enough milk this can lead to quite a few issues, including feeding aversion (see page 159).

Expressing breast milk

Ideally, you should only express breast milk (or pump) when you have a premature or sick baby, or a very low weight baby. Expressing or pumping breast milk is the only way to maintain lactation when the baby and mother are separated by illness, low weight or prematurity.

The problem as I see it today is that *all* women are educated to—and are expected to—express or pump, even when they have a healthy baby. Midwives start from day one hand-expressing 1–2 mls of colostrum from the new mother rather than sitting with them, helping and encouraging them to attach their baby to the breast. It takes time for a new mother to learn and as a midwife we should teach the mother the skills she needs to assist the baby herself (rather than have midwives pushing the baby onto the breast). A breast pump is the top of the 'to buy' list and if you walk around a maternity ward you will see a breast pump outside every room.

It is 100 per cent possible to breastfeed your baby without expressing at all. Expressing milk day in and day out is causing a community of anxious and obsessive mothers. Anxious because they have such little time in the day to themselves anyway and they are always trying to achieve a volume of milk, and obsessive as they constantly sit on a breast pump to express milk. This is not what Mother Nature intended. Some women are advised before leaving the hospital (with a well baby) to hire a pump for months, at great expense. All this expressing takes precious time away from attaching, holding and loving their newborn baby. The lactating brain works beautifully when it has a baby sucking at the nipple, calm in his mother's arms, with his mother looking at him with love and affection.

If a mother with a *well baby* expresses and sees that the volume of expressed milk decreases over the days, weeks and months, she thinks she is not lactating properly. In my experience she is more likely to give up breastfeeding as she thinks she doesn't have enough milk.

If expressing because of a premature baby or a sick baby, the most important thing is to express even the smallest amount to get the milk moving. When the baby is old enough and strong enough to attach to the breast, the milk supply will increase.

When is expressing not necessary?
Expressing milk is not necessary if you have a well baby, your baby is attaching to the breast properly and you are feeding well. Unnecessary expressing of the breasts leads to:

- unnecessary time away from your baby
- thinking expressing will increase your milk supply

- anxiety as you are trying to make a 'volume' of breast milk
- keeping you home and 'attached' to a pump
- dreading pumping.

Time and again, I see women expressing or pumping, feeding babies with cups rather than having the baby suck at the breast, which is best for the mother, the baby and the mother's lactation. I find it all so confusing that midwives, lactation consultants and maternal and child health nurses all want the same thing, but we are giving mixed messages to our most vulnerable new mothers. I'm not sure if it's just the time factor in the hospital, where the midwives do not have the time to sit with new mums and explain how lactation works, or if it's just routine to express breast milk from day one. In my view, it is just not necessary.

Week 1 was tough. It's all about calories. We top him up with formula, but as Cath explains, he is just so little and we need to 'fill up his legs'. She changed our perception about formula and breastfeeding. Breastfeeding is the goal, and we will get there, it's just a different path. As Max gets bigger it should be easier for him to attach and not fall asleep after ten minutes of sucking.

Breastfeeding is hard. The more you talk about it with others, the more you find out how hard it was for most people. It just so happens that our best friends had no trouble with it so we were kind of expecting the same.

SAM

Situations when you should express	Situations when you don't need to express
Premature baby	To stimulate your milk supply
Sick baby after birth at any age if he is unable to suck	To supplement your breast milk
Baby who needs care in a special care nursery	If you have sore or cracked nipples
Severe shooting pain up your breast	If you have engorged or full breasts
When you are weaning and need to express for comfort	If you have flat or inverted nipples
Baby who is losing weight and needs formula feeds	

Breastfeeding premature babies

Babies who need care in the special care nursery because of prematurity, infection, low blood sugar or breathing difficulties often cannot be breastfed.

If you have a premature baby, expressing every three hours during the day and providing as much milk as you can is vital for the little one. Depending on the prematurity of the baby, his age and weight, medical staff will calculate how much breast milk the baby requires. Women who have excess breast milk can store and freeze it and bring it into hospital as required for the baby.

As the baby grows he will need more breast milk, so don't be surprised if at some point you cannot keep up with the demand. The nursery staff will give the baby formula as a top-up. Once the baby is sucking on your breast 24/7 your lactation will increase.

If you go home and your baby needs to stay in hospital, I suggest you do the following:

- express three-hourly during the day for fifteen minutes on each side
- do your last expressing at around 11 pm
- sleep overnight
- wake at 5–6 am and express.

I find it is beneficial for the new mum to have a good stretch of sleep overnight if she is travelling in and out of the hospital, as it is a very tiring and emotional time for all. Some midwives advise mothers to get up at 3 am to express, but I think you are better off sleeping for six hours. You won't have less milk, you won't get mastitis and you will feel you can cope with the daily visits to the hospital and all that entails.

Kylie's story

Over 33 years ago I delivered a baby named Kylie, who was born at 32 weeks. I fed her daily through a gavage tube as she was too little and too tired to begin sucking at the breast or take a bottle. Her mum Gwen, once home, would express five times a day and bring the milk into the hospital for Kylie. I can remember that at times she would only express 5–10 ml at a time and no more than 100 ml a day. I encouraged her to keep going and not worry about the amount she expressed, and reassured her once Kylie was on the breast Gwen's lactation would increase.

When Kylie was older and strong enough to attach to the breast she sucked well.

After discharge I kept in contact with Gwen and her family and she breastfed Kylie for fifteen months. I have just recently delivered Kylie's second baby . . . talk about the circle of life, I'm now delivering my baby's babies!

This story is to encourage any mum who has a premature or sick baby and needs to express. Keep going even if you get 5 mls each time you express. Once the baby is strong enough and is on your breast, your very clever body, along with Mother Nature, will ensure you breastfeed for as long as you wish.

Bottles and formula

Most new mums want to breastfeed, but there are so many reasons why the formula option is necessary. Not everyone lactates the same way and not everyone has the capacity to breastfeed. Sometimes babies are born prematurely with a limited reflex to suck and may need a bottle in the early days to ensure good and consistent weight gain. Some mums wish to bottle-feed from birth for personal reasons. Bottle-feeding is not a reflection on how good a parent is. It's not about the milk, it's the parenting that is important.

If the baby had used formula while in hospital, most new parents will continue with the same formula. If the baby begins formula-feeding after hospital the choice recommendations often come from professionals and friends. If there is any reaction to the initial formula used with the advice of an MCH nurse or a paediatrician, you can change the formula. It is important not to change the formula without medical advice—do not give a baby a different formula based on Google or girlfriends' recommendations!

You must be organised when you bottle-feed a baby. You will need a reliable electric steriliser, six to eight bottles, plus a bottle-cleaner to ensure the bottles and teats are washed properly after each use and before sterilising. A large plastic container placed in the fridge can be used to hold all the sterilised bottles—this way, the bottles stay clean and sterile.

The fridge will decrease the risk of any bacteria growing inside warm, moist bottles.

To bottle-feed a baby, cradle the baby in your left arm and hold the bottle at a 45-degree angle in your right hand. In the early weeks I would wrap the baby so he feels secure. Place the teat near the baby's mouth and as the baby opens his mouth gently allow the baby to suck the teat in. Ensure the inside of the teat is full of milk during feeding.

If milk is dribbling out the side of the baby's mouth it is usually because the lid on the bottle has not been firmly applied. Babies do not take in air while bottle-feeding if the bottle is given to the baby at such an angle that the inside of the teat is full of milk. Babies gulp breast milk too, so don't worry too much if your baby gulps while he is bottle-feeding; babies are very clever and will only drink as much as they can cope with, in a manner that suits them. Sometimes a baby will put his tongue up on his top palate and, even though you have the bottle in his mouth, you need to ensure his tongue is down as that is the only way he will successfully feed.

Babies who use a bottle at some feeds will not get nipple confusion when breastfeeding. Babies never refuse the breast but will refuse a bottle if they have not been given a bottle within the first four to six weeks. Often they will continue to refuse a bottle completely.

If you wish to offer your baby a bottle while breastfeeding, the answer is to offer it in the first few weeks after birth. There are so many variables on how much you give a baby it's impossible to give one-size-fits-all advice. It depends on the age, weight and maturity of the baby, so consult your paediatrician or MCH nurse.

Formula-feeding your baby

I am a strong advocate for breastfeeding and encourage women to breastfeed their babies for up to and beyond a year, but there are plenty of situations where formula is necessary. Also, some women don't want to breastfeed. Some mums cannot breastfeed their babies. Some mums don't have enough milk to sustain a good weight for their babies. How they feed their child is their choice and right, and we must respect and support them, not make them feel like they are poisoning their baby with a safe product. As a society, we have become a little intolerant of mums who don't want, or choose not, to breastfeed. Making a new mother feel guilty about not breastfeeding is just cruel.

We all know that breast is best, and so do the mums who cannot breastfeed their babies. It's one of the hardest and most emotional decisions that a woman can make, and I always want to support the mother to be happy and healthy, so she can be a good mum to her children.

I am old enough to have worked in hospitals when the woman who had the most breast milk in the ward would share her supply with the women who didn't have enough or would help feed the premature babies in the nursery. Those days are behind us, so our only alternative is formula, which is food made for babies.

Most mums come to parenthood thinking that breast-feeding is actually easy, but if you worked with me for just one day you would see the many issues I encounter around breastfeeding. Times have changed and so has the generation that we are caring for now. I've had to change my practice and be more flexible to introduce formula at times when I know that the mother does not, or cannot, breastfeed.

The bath, bottle and bed (BBB) routine that I invented gets the dad or partner to bath the baby at 10 pm, dress him, wrap him and give him a bottle of formula. This routine allows the mum to breastfeed the baby right up until bath time and then she goes to bed. (For more information, see page 129.)

I often ask new mums who are upset about giving the baby top-up formula, 'What is your alternative?' Formula is the only option. Pumping is not sustainable, it is not natural and causes anxiety and distress to mothers. Medications do not help either and can sometimes give new mothers the false hope that they will lactate more.

Formula myths

Formula is baby food, so enough already of making our new mothers feel guilty about giving babies formula. Food Standards Australia New Zealand is considering placing a 'warning' on tins of formula about the risks to infant health of not breastfeeding.

Breastfeeding rates will rise if we present new parents with guilt-free information—that includes giving formula to babies who are hungry or in need of extra kilojoules (calories). Giving formula will not reduce the supply of breast milk or confuse a baby. It's all food, and women will breastfeed longer if they give some formula to babies who require added kilojoules (calories) in the early weeks.

Formula 101

If you are fully bottle-feeding it is really important to be organised. Earlier I recommended having an electric steriliser, plus six to eight bottles and your formula. If you plan to only bottle-feed or the baby needs some extra formula top-ups, I suggest you buy a new kettle that is just for the baby's water.

You can make up a bottle each time the baby wakes up. Remember that if you are using boiled water that has cooled down, it may still be too warm for the baby who has woken up crying and is very impatient for food.

You can also make up the bottles with just water and put them in the fridge. Then when it's time for the baby to be fed, you can warm the water and add the correct amount of formula, shake the bottle properly so all the powder dissolves in the water, and test on your forearm that the milk is at body temperature.

To do this, put your arm out and tip a few drops of the formula on your wrist (remember not to let the teat touch your skin). If the formula feels cold on your skin it's too cold for the baby; if the formula feels hot on your skin it's too hot for the baby. If you don't feel the formula on your skin it is the correct temperature.

Another method is to make a jug of boiled water that will cover a 24-hour period of feeding. I suggest you use a glass jug that has a lid (if not, put some plastic wrap or tinfoil over the jug). It's a good idea to boil the water first thing in the morning and keep the sterilised bottles in the fridge.

I suggest you make up 200 mls more than you think your baby would normally have in 24 hours. So, if your baby is having 800 mls a day, make up a litre. Always keep the jug of water in the fridge and only take it out to fill up the bottles. Discard any remaining water the next morning and make a new batch for the new day.

How to prepare formula

- Wash the bottle in hot soapy water and rinse with hot water from the tap.
- Stand the bottle in the sink and fill it with just boiled water.
- Boil the kettle again.
- Pour the water out of the bottle and refill with the correct amount of boiling water, then add the correct number of scoops of formula.
- Put the formula in the bottle and thoroughly mix the powder and water together. Place the lid or a cover on the bottle and refrigerate immediately.
- Each time you need to feed the baby pour the selected amount of formula into the sterilised bottle and heat the bottle of milk.
- You can heat the bottle by either using a bottle warmer, or standing the bottle in a mug of hot water.
- Always shake the bottle before you give it to the baby to ensure that the formula is the correct temperature. Unused formula in each bottle must be thrown out.

FAQs about formula

Will the mother have to express her milk?

No. As the mother has breastfed the baby until bath time, her brain does not know her baby is having a bottle of formula.

When the baby wakes up her breasts will be full and she will certainly be ready to feed the baby. One mother asked me whether her breasts will explode—I reassured her they wouldn't!

Will the bottle of formula turn the baby away from the breast?

No. Babies are very, very clever and will never refuse the breast. One formula a day—even seven formulas a day after a breastfeed—will not take the baby away from the breast.

There is no such thing as nipple confusion. Confusion only occurs if you do not offer a baby a bottle from the early weeks—he will then totally refuse a bottle from eight weeks onwards and exclusively breastfeed. You should start the bottle from the first night you come home from hospital, along with the bath routine.

I speak to many mums who call to say the baby will not take a bottle at three, four months and after. They want to give the baby a bottle as they have reasons such as returning to work or attending a special occasion.

What formula is best?

All hospitals use formulas, especially for the premature babies. I suggest you ask the midwives in the hospital what formula they use and go by that.

Why can't I use expressed breast milk?

You can. To use expressed breast milk you need to pump at least twice a day to get the volume of milk you will need for your baby after the bath. This can add extra anxiety to your day. The whole concept around the bath and bottle routine is to give the mother a well-deserved physical and emotional break from the baby. It also gives the partner precious time bathing the baby, and giving the baby a bottle allows the partner hands-on time with the baby.

Wee and poo

Until you have a baby, you won't believe how much they poo. You wonder where it's all coming from; the consistency and the sounds are enormous. It reflects that you are feeding well and passing this on to your baby, so be proud. As I say, compliments to the chef!

Your baby's first bowel motion is called meconium. Stored in the baby's bowel since life in utero, meconium is thick, sterile, black and sticky, with no smell. As the breast milk or formula goes through the system, the bowel action changes in consistency and colour from the black meconium to a dark green transitional poo. Then, as more breast milk goes through the system, the poo becomes runny, yellow . . . and frequent!

There are a few times you should be concerned about the baby's bowel actions. That is, when it's black, red or white. Black (meconium is the exception) could mean the baby has some internal bleeding high in the gut. Red poo may mean an allergy to cow's milk protein, or a bowel complication called intussusception (when the bowel telescopes in on itself and the baby has 'redcurrant jelly' poo). White poo is when the baby's liver is not producing enough bile, or if the flow of bile is blocked and not draining from the liver, leaving the baby's poo pale, grey or clay-coloured. In all of these situations you must seek medical advice. Take a photo of the soiled nappy and put the nappy in a plastic bag to show the doctor.

A fully breastfed baby will have runny, yellow poo and they can poo before, during and after every feed. Some breastfed babies can go for more than ten days without a poo. A breastfed baby is never constipated, so continue to feed and as long as the baby is passing wind, the poo will follow.

A baby also needs to pass lots of urine so we need plenty of wet nappies with a new baby. This means he is well hydrated. If your baby's nappies are dry or your baby has not passed urine, you need to seek medical advice and have the baby checked by a doctor.

Your baby may need some extra milk to help correct his fluid balance. If the baby is drinking well and hydrated his urine will be clear. If he is low in fluid his urine will be dark and a concentrated dark yellow, often with urates, which stain the nappy with orange crystals. If this is the case the baby needs some more breast milk to rehydrate. Never give a baby water, or water with sugar.

Blood in the baby's poo

Cow's milk protein is one of the most common causes of food allergies in newborn babies. You will notice blood in the baby's poo and you should either take a photo of the blood-stained poo or take the nappy with you when you see the doctor. Some people might find it offputting, but it's amazing what you do for your own child. If you are breastfeeding, the paediatrician will encourage you to eliminate all dairy products from your diet. If your child is allergic to cow's milk, avoid milk and all milk-containing foods.

If the baby continues to have blood in his poo, your paediatrician will advise you to start the baby on a prescription formula and express your milk until the baby's bowel actions settle down. Just so you know, the prescription formula smells foul (and so does the baby's poo) but the babies drink it happily enough. Forewarned is forearmed.

If the baby has any signs of gastroenteritis, the doctor may order a sample of the baby's poo to be sent to pathology for testing.

The baby's weight

I worry about a baby when he loses weight and does so consistently. For the first four to five days after birth the baby may lose up to 10 per cent of his birth weight. But once lactation is established, and if formula top-ups are given or if the baby is fully formula-fed, the baby will not lose that much weight and in fact may leave hospital having gained weight.

The average weight gain for a baby who is over a week old and feeding well is 100–150 grams per week. All babies are different: some put on 50–70 grams per week and some might put on 300 grams. Both are normal if the weight gain is consistent and the baby follows its percentile growth. If a baby becomes sick during the first six weeks the first thing he will refuse is milk, so seek medical advice quickly for a baby younger than six weeks.

Don't be surprised if the baby's weight gain is not consistent during the weekly weigh-ins with your maternal and child health nurse. Depending on age and activity, each baby puts on different amounts weekly. Your baby cannot put on too much weight while breastfeeding or on formula milk.

Obesity starts if incorrect fatty foods are given in early childhood so if you have a bottle-fed or breastfed baby who has lots of fat rolls on his arms and legs and tummy, be thankful for a healthy and well-fed baby. Ignore snide remarks about your baby being overweight. When your child turns two he will run around and burn off his fat stores.

As your breast milk increases, so will your baby's sucking and his weight gain. This varies from baby to baby, and babies put on a different amount of weight each week. If your baby is losing weight and losing weight consistently, you need to seek professional advice.

The percentile growth chart that you'll find in your baby's health book compares a child's weight, height and head circumference to other children of the same age and sex to assess where your baby is placed on the growth chart. Plotting your baby's measurements will give you a general idea how he is developing physically. The chart also gives your doctor or MCH nurse an overall indication that your baby is growing as he should be.

When comparing 100 babies of the same age on the percentile charts, if a baby is on the tenth percentile for weight, it means that 90 per cent of other babies at the same age weigh more and are longer in length than this baby. A baby on the sixtieth percentile for height and weight is taller and heavier than 60 per cent of other babies.

The hungry baby

A hungry baby does not sleep! So many new parents contact me, saying that the baby is crying and upset, has bad wind, colic or anything else that Google and girlfriends have advised them.

In most cases, the crying baby is just hungry. Feed him. I'll keep reminding you throughout the book: you cannot overfeed a baby but you can underfeed a baby. Boys are always hungry, so if you have a baby boy remember there are times when you just can't seem to fill them, especially if his dad is 1.9 metres tall.

A hungry baby is awake, crying, searching with his mouth open from side to side, looking for a nipple to suck. He is well, but he is hungry. A baby who is hungry needs either breast milk or, if he has sucked long enough at the breast, a formula top-up. You will see the difference with the baby once he has had a drink—he will sleep.

Be careful not to replace milk with a dummy for a dummy does not have any kilojoules (calories). It may settle the baby and stop him crying as the baby sucks vigorously on the dummy, but it will not give him any food to help him grow, settle and be a happy baby who thrives and eventually sleeps well. A dummy can be used to settle the baby to sleep once he has had enough to drink.

The crying baby

Crying is a normal part of the baby's development. Some babies cry a lot, and even though you are aware that babies cry before you have one, there is nothing more disturbing than *your* baby crying at length, and when you are unable to stop or settle him. Often babies start crying more at about two weeks of age and may continue until about twelve weeks of age. All babies tend to go through a period of crying.

I hear from many women that they are unprepared as well as disturbed and distressed by a crying baby. We all feel the same. This can be worse if you are with your new baby and everybody's staring at you—you really feel so bad. (I always go up to mothers in the supermarket and shops with crying babies and say, 'Don't worry, the crying is only worrying you, just keep smiling and get home as soon as you can.')

My son cried for months due to reflux, which was very distressing. I knew he was not sick, since he was growing rapidly and I had lots of breast milk. But still he cried. I can remember walking with my friend Claire daily, and her son Tom would sleep for the whole walk and I would be carrying Lachlan and pushing the pram because as soon as I put him down he would start crying. The good news is, he is a perfectly healthy 22-year-old now, but I still remember the constant crying, and how hard it was as a new parent.

Google, girlfriends, family and friends will start diagnosing your baby with colic, a generic word that everybody uses when a baby cries constantly. They will tell you if the baby is pulling his legs up he is in pain and it's colic. Remember: if your baby is in such pain, he would be sick.

The really difficult thing with a crying baby is that you feel totally responsible, inadequate, guilty and sometimes ashamed that you cannot stop your own baby from crying. The baby looks like he's in pain because when he cries his face screws up, he pulls his legs up like he has bad bowel spasms, and before you know it, you are at the GP or local hospital. Then when you arrive at the doctor's, your baby miraculously starts to smile, blows raspberries and looks like the happiest baby in the world.

I can remember, instead of putting a sheet on my son's bed, I used to put on one of my T-shirts, hoping that my smell would help him go to sleep. You really do try anything.

Opposite is a checkbox to reassure you that a baby crying in the first six months of life, even when it seems never to stop, is normal.

The crying game

C	R	Y	I	N	G
Crying that never seems to stop	Relatives tell you it's colic or wind	Your baby never seems happy	The baby looks like he is in pain	Afternoon and night-time is worse	Goes from 2 weeks to 12 weeks

C The crying never seems to stop. You are sure none of your friends ever had babies who cried as much as your baby. The truth is, they probably did.

R All your relatives constantly comment on the baby's crying. They say 'it must be colic' or 'you don't have enough milk'. Nothing helpful is offered to you.

Y Your baby never seems happy. At mothers' group you walk around with vomit dripping off you, but all the other mums are in black jeans with not a drop of vomit on them.

I The baby looks like he is in pain. His face screws up. What's all this about happy, smiling babies?

N Nights are the worst. As soon as dinner is served the baby cries. Your partner is feeding you while you feed your baby. This wasn't in the vows.

G This seems to go on for a lifetime but it does stop at around twelve weeks, so circle the magic date!

It saddens me to listen to parents who get angry at a crying baby. I've even heard parents describe their crying baby as 'naughty'. Let's stop for a minute and think about what we are saying. A baby is not choosing to cry. For goodness sake, he is a *baby*. It's important not to assume your baby has motivations that only someone much older could be capable of. If, as a parent, you're feeling overwhelmed and unable to cope, reach out to get the support you need. See 'Your emotions' on page 210 where I look at emotional changes after childbirth and 'Seeking help' on page 271.

It's usual to feel terrible in such a situation. You look at all your friends and around your mothers' group and all their babies are on the floor laughing, kicking their legs, and all you do is walk around holding your crying baby. Again. You look at those women, thinking, how do they do it—my baby just cries all the time. You walk away wondering what is wrong with you and your baby, he never seems happy—and to top if off, he cries the whole way home.

Then that horrible clock on the wall strikes six and the crying *worsens*. As it escalates you walk around the house, feed your baby, put on the white noise that is supposed to soothe every baby. Nothing works.

On really desperate nights you send your partner out driving with the baby. He is gone for hours and hours, driving around the city and suburbs, and the baby sleeps soundly in the car. As soon as he pulls into your driveway the baby starts crying, so off he goes again for another circuit. Even your partner thinks he's going mad and tells his workmates how he drove around to stop the baby crying. Luckily his fellow workmates just laugh and agree with him—they have all been there, done that, got the T-shirt.

You watch TV and read magazines (on the toilet, as that is the only free time you have) and notice how all the celebrities have perfect babies and go out all dressed in white. The mother and baby look so calm. *How?*, you ask yourself.

You look back at the photos of your new baby while you were in hospital and you are holding a calm, quiet little baby—what has happened? All he has done is scream and cry in between some happy times. Sometimes you feel even more insecure as a mother because everyone else seems able to calm your baby except you.

That's the bad news.

The good news is, the baby will get better and stop crying. He will grow out of it. Here are some positive steps you can take to help you and your family through this period.

Midwife Cath's survival tips for a crying baby

- Have your baby checked to ensure that he is not unwell.
- Feed your baby.
- Love your baby.
- When visiting your paediatrician or your MCH nurse, eliminate gastric reflux (page 165) and/or cow's milk protein allergy (page 107).

- If the baby has reflux use medication by script, *not* over-the-counter drops.
- Hold your baby upright as much as you can.
- Get up and have a shower every morning.
- Get dressed even if it's very early, before your partner leaves for work.
- Discuss with your partner how you are feeling and how he can help.
- Make sure you are organised around the house and have help with cooking, cleaning and washing.
- If you feel angry and anxious, put the baby safely in the cot and walk away for a few minutes. Take a deep breath and regroup before you go and hold your baby again.
- Remember your baby is not doing this to hurt you or upset you.
- Realise he's not angry, grumpy or doing this on purpose—he's only a baby.
- Make sure he is not crying from a wet or dirty nappy.
- Enlist support from your mum, mother-in-law and good friends.
- Don't try and problem-solve what is wrong with your baby; look on him as a well baby.
- Buy a baby carrier that can hold your baby close to you and upright, as you will be walking a lot with him.

- Buy a dummy—sometimes crying babies need the comfort of a dummy after they have been fed.
- Don't attend new mothers' groups if you are feeling vulnerable and your baby is the only one who cries a lot.
- Ring a friend and go for a walk every day.
- When your partner comes home, have a bath or shower or lie down on the bed and take 15–30 minutes of quiet time to yourself.

One of the first things to learn as a new parent is *patience*, which you will need as long as you are parenting. From new baby to toddler, kindergarten to school and the teenage years, all children require very patient parents.

Week 1

Feed, play and sleep routine

Bath, bottle and bed

From the first night home start the bath, bottle and bed (BBB) routine (see page 129). It's great if the mums can go to bed around 9.45 pm after feeding the baby, but I find it takes a few days for new mums not to 'hover' over their very capable partners.

Initally every baby is going to sleep for different lengths of time after the bath and bottle but as he gains weight and gets older week by week, the length of time he sleeps will increase. Initially the length of his sleep depends on his weight at birth and how much he weighs after leaving hospital. Every newborn baby has at least one good stretch of sleep and the bath helps 'train' the baby to have that long stretch of sleep after 11 pm. If you can all sleep through from 11 pm to 2 am that will prevent the debilitating 'jetlag' sleep-deprivation feeling.

The first week you may find he sleeps for two to three hours after the bath. This is normal. When he wakes, pick him up and feed him. Offer him one side or half the bottle (if you are formula-feeding). When finished, unwrap the baby, change his nappy, burp him, rewrap and feed again on the other side or give him the rest of the bottle. Then, lots of kisses and cuddles, and put him down to sleep. If he wakes again, pick him up and feed him again—remember he needs lots of kilojoules (calories) in these first weeks and months, and you can't overfeed a baby.

When he wakes up again, pick him up, feed, unwrap halfway through and change him, then rewrap and feed again. In the first week the feed may take up to two hours. This feels abnormal but the 2–3 hourly feeds will increase to 3–4 hourly as the baby gains weight. He may still have his days and nights mixed up, so be patient, it gets better!

Some professionals insist that new mothers don't have any eye contact with their baby overnight so they won't 'overstimulate him'. I find this so sad that mothers are discouraged from looking at and loving their baby in case they don't sleep.

Love your baby. Have eye contact with him overnight; he may even smile at you. These night feeds together with your new baby are short and precious: look at him, love him and tell him just how much he means to you.

Smelly necks, underarms and behind the ears

When you bath your baby there are a few spots you should ensure you keep clean and dry. As babies seem to have more rolls of skin under their chin and no neck, moisture gets trapped between the folds, which can result in a moist and smelly rash. In the first weeks the baby may still have some vernix in his armpit—as you bath him make sure his underarm is clean and pat dry well. Apply a little nappy-rash powder to keep the folds of the skin dry. The powder absorbs moisture quickly and also helps prevent chafing.

Often babies posset a little milk when sleeping or lying with their head on the side. When this happens day after day a build-up of dry milk can pool behind the ears and lobes. Ensure you wash the baby's earlobes with some pure soap and dry behind his ears. A small amount of nappy-rash powder will help if there is any chaffing.

Daytime feeds

Daytime with the baby during the first seven days changes only very little. At birth the baby can be really sleepy, perhaps from jaundice, or as he naturally hibernates. Babies are known for having their days and nights confused, which means they are perfect during the day and party like it's 1999 at night.

When born their routine stays the same and if you think about it, that is all babies know. So you will notice a quiet and restful, sleepy baby during the day and an alert and wakeful baby who won't go to sleep overnight. Don't panic—you need to go with the flow and be prepared for these long nights when you wonder if this baby is ever going to sleep. The late bath helps, but it takes about two weeks for the baby to change his days and nights around to a more normal sleep time.

Daytime feeds are usually every three hours during the day, with the week-old baby happily going back to sleep. Wake the baby after three hours' sleep during the day as he may go into a four- to five-hour sleep that you would rather happen overnight.

Take the time of his feeds from the end of the feed. So if the baby stops feeding and goes to sleep at midday, wake him up at 3 pm for his next feed. If you take it from the beginning of the feed and the baby takes 1½ hours to feed, the baby only sleeps for 1½ hours and is not ready or alert enough to feed. Believe me, if he is hungry a baby will wake up for feeds before the three hours. A baby needs plenty of feeds/kilojoules (calories) during the day, right up to the bath time when he can have his bath and bottle.

Try not to overuse a dummy as it has no kilojoules (calories). A dummy is fantastic in the first six weeks if you have fed the baby, he has reflux, and he is squirming a lot. A baby never uses *you* as a dummy as he gets milk from you whenever he sucks.

Play

It's so important to start floor time with your baby in the first week during the daytime. Begin with a few minutes of tummy time and back time, and in between each side you feed. Put a nice rug on the floor so the baby is warm and comfortable. Play during the first week does not need to be longer than

3–5 minutes each time. Watch him lift his head while on his tummy: he will lift it and turn his head from side to side and you will be amazed at just how clever and strong your newborn baby is at such a young age. His head movement looks frantic but in fact his primitive 'rooting reflex' is telling him to search for the nipple so he can suck and feed. Clever, isn't he?

By the end of week one . . .

- The council/community maternal and child health nurse (MCH) will do a home visit and weigh your baby.
- Your breasts are feeling full but comfortable, with no red areas. However, they may become engorged and your nipples may be grazed or cracked.
- Your blood loss is slight, and a mucusy red in colour.
- You should be passing urine with no pain.
- Make sure you have a bowel movement each day. Even though you may be scared about having one, believe me, nothing will tear, even though it feels as if it might.
- Keep your fluids up and eat well. You are feeding another person so you need to drink a lot of fluids and take time to eat.
- Remember that you need to look after yourself so you can look after your baby.

- Your baby is very noisy at night, and makes lots of weird grunts and groans. It's very likely that you'll experience the baby blues around day two or three. See page 210.
- He may gag or vomit after some feeds.
- He has a lot of wind (that is not harmful).

Feeding chart

At the end of each chapter, from chapters 4 to 9, I have included a feeding chart so you can record your baby's feeding times, the number of his wet and dirty nappies, the amount of formula you've given him, and his sleep times. These charts will become a keepsake of your baby's first six weeks. You'll find the first chart on the following page.

Feeding chart

Date and time	Breast (mins)		Formula (mls)	Nappy		Sleep (mins)	Comments
	Left	Right		Wet	Pooey		
18-Apr-16 12:41pm	3	4	180	✓	—	105	Settled easily

Feeding chart

Date and time	Breast (mins)		Formula (mls)	Nappy		Sleep (mins)	Comments
	Left	Right		Wet	Pooey		
18-Apr-16 12:41pm	3	4	180	✓	—	105	Settled easily

Feeding chart

Date and time	Breast (mins)		Formula (mls)	Nappy		Sleep (mins)	Comments
	Left	Right		Wet	Pooey		
18-Apr-16 12:41pm	3	4	180	✓	—	105	Settled easily

5

Week two

You've celebrated your first week as parents. Congratulations! You can't believe you survived the week, nor can you imagine your life without this little person next to you, growing in front of you, making such loud grunting noises, squirming all night, keeping you awake while he is asleep, then very quiet during the day. But it's all worth it.

I was worried about Max sleeping on us while we were lounging on the couch. I didn't want him to get in a bad habit. You hear that a lot, don't let them get into bad habits, but Cath reminds us he is only two weeks old, and you can't give him enough love. Another mind-twisting statement. You can't give him enough love. If he wants to sleep on us for the first bit of his life, then I am happy to provide. As the other parent, this was our special time. I am guilt-free for having my little breathing, warm, sleeping son on my chest.

SAM

This week, you may wonder where your quiet, sleepy baby went. Suddenly you have a baby who's looking around and crying endlessly for food. Don't regard your baby as being unsettled all the time, think of him as hungry and growing, and to grow he needs food—and a lot of it, constantly.

Babies need to weigh at least 8 to 9 kilograms before they have the capacity to sleep a decent stretch overnight. However, if your baby is not wakeful and is too sleepy, jaundiced and not feeding well, you need to seek medical advice.

For your baby to gain weight, you need to feed him frequently in the first six weeks. Some baby books have you thinking that the baby needs to be sleeping up to eighteen hours a day. No, they don't. They can't. A baby needs to feed to put on weight, and to do this the baby has to be awake so he can be fed regularly.

A few golden rules

- You *cannot* overfeed a baby.
- You *can* underfeed a baby.
- Breast milk or formula is the main source of food for the baby's first twelve months.
- Healthy, well babies who are born at term cry for two reasons: hunger and discomfort. The discomfort is usually associated with gastric reflux (see page 165) or cow's milk protein allergy (see page 107).

- Babies need to be at least 8 to 9 kilograms to have the capacity to sleep a good stretch overnight.
- Babies need to be old enough to have the capacity to sleep well overnight.
- A newborn baby cannot self-settle and needs to feed to sleep.
- Don't let a young baby cry for long periods in his cot.
- Pick him up, carry him, love him, talk to him.

The bath, bottle and bed (BBB) routine

Many years ago I developed the bath, bottle and bed routine for newborn babies. I encourage new parents to get into one routine from the first night they come home from hospital. Some people set themselves such a strict routine that they can't possibly stick to it and put so much pressure on themselves that it all becomes too much, often ending in tears for everyone!

My advice is to bath the baby at around 10 pm *every* night. The worst time to bath a newborn baby is 6 pm as the bath relaxes the baby. I want the newborn baby to start sleeping his long stretch of time after 11 pm. Some professionals advise new parents to bath their baby every second day or only once a week. Babies need a bath every night. The bath is the beginning of a routine that lasts a lifetime.

Having a baby brought a great deal of joy to our lives and certainly changed our daily routines and the freedom we once had. With Kylie feeding baby Leo and looking after him most of the day we decided that I should give him a late bath followed by a bottle so as to spend more time together and to give Kylie some rest.

Knowing that Leo could take a bottle without having to rely on Kylie was also beneficial, particularly when unexpected circumstances arose and having a bottle was necessary. His bath was slowly brought forward to 6 pm and it is a routine we still follow almost two years later.

MARK

In the early days, bathing your baby at night helps him relax, just like when we have a bath after a full day's work. (See page 133 for bathing.) I suggest your partner does the bathing, with the mother going to bed at 9.30–9.45 pm. The ultimate aim is to get your baby sleeping from the 10 pm bath and bottle to 3 or 4 am. That is our jetlag time and when you feel like no one else in the world is awake. If you are parenting alone follow the same routine and, if possible, enlist a group of trusted people who can come around and bath the baby, give him a bottle and settle him to sleep for you.

After the baby's bath at 10 pm he is wrapped and given a bottle of formula, then put to bed. When the baby next wakes, which should be around 2 to 3 am, the mother breastfeeds the baby, which may take up to an hour and a half. This is usually the only overnight feed that's needed. The partner goes to bed for the night after the bath and bottle—you only need one tired person in the household.

When following this routine all the mothers say to me how fabulous they feel having some emotional and physical time away from the baby, time for a deep sleep of four hours' duration, sometimes even five. Sleep makes you able to cope with the long days and weeks ahead. The partner also sleeps well and is off-duty until the morning.

All the women I work with who follow this routine seem to breastfeed longer, for well over twelve months. Their short break from the baby, being able to sleep for over three hours and working with their partner as a team results in a more harmonious household. Plus there's a happy, well-fed baby too!

Can you see the team working together now?

You're working in the home during the day, feeding and looking after your baby, while your partner is at work. Then, when your partner comes home, you feed the baby, have dinner, and at 10 pm your partner baths the baby, gives him a bottle and puts the baby to bed.

This is a fabulous time for your partner, who can bond with the baby while you're asleep. Then you get up and feed your baby the next time he wakes which, ultimately, is between 3 and 4 am. This way, you're sleeping from 10 pm or before until the baby wakes. Please note: your breasts will not 'explode', you do not need to express, and when you wake you will have full breasts ready to feed.

As the baby gains weight, gets older and sleeps longer past midnight and towards 2, 3, 4 and 5 am, I encourage you to slowly bring the bath forward in 30-minute increments over the next six to ten weeks. The 10 pm bath won't be forever.

By about eight to nine weeks old, you bath him at 9.30 pm, then 9 pm, and by the time your baby is about three to four months old, he'll have a bath at about 6 pm, have a feed and go to bed. Then you introduce the 'dream' or 'roll over feed' at 10 pm when the baby is asleep. (See page 133 for more on the dream feed.)

Being an organised person, I struggled most with the fact that I couldn't just fall into the pattern I wanted, and which I thought was a fairly flexible one pre-delivery. Babies challenge you in many ways. I had to teach myself to relax and go with the flow, but more importantly I had to learn to cut myself some slack. Accept help when it's offered and use the down time not to do chores but to unwind doing something for you—go for a walk/read a book. Having Cath provide us with guidance and support was invaluable to us in starting, settling and establishing ourselves into the new world of parenthood. When it comes to babies, forewarned is definitely forearmed!

SIMONE AND MARK

The dream feed or rollover feed

A dream feed occurs when your baby is six months or weighs 8 to 9 kilograms, and you give him a bottle or breastfeed at night while he is asleep. The baby goes to bed at 6–7 pm after a feed, then at 10 pm every night you pick him up when he is asleep and feed him, still wrapped and asleep, till he is about ten months old. Once fed, burped, kissed and cuddled, put the sleepy baby back to bed . . . hopefully for a long sleep for all of you.

The dream feed tops him up with milk so he stays asleep over the early hours of 1 am to 4 am. Your partner can do the dream feed while you sleep or you may wish to breastfeed your baby for the dream feed—it's up to you. I breastfed fully and enjoyed the experience immensely. But today I find both parents want to be involved with feeding the baby.

There is no scientific evidence to say that your baby will not take a nipple after he's given a bottle. In fact, it is helpful if your baby will take both breast and bottle, especially when the time comes to weaning the baby or going back to work.

Bathing your baby Midwife Cath-style

Bathing your baby can be a wonderful experience for both you and the baby. The first thing to do is to have everything organised. Have the bath filled with warm water, deep enough so it comes up to your baby's neck. Test the water temperature.

Have clean towels and face washers, some nappies, a clean singlet and onesie for the baby. Bath your baby every night and *do not* shower your baby—it is dangerous and the adult could easily fall or the baby slip. A bath is calming, warm and relaxing.

First you undress your baby, but leave the nappy on just in case. Wrap your baby up in a towel and hold your baby under your arm so his head is just being tilted over the bath, as if he is about to be baptised. Use a face washer to gently rub around his head.

This practice ensures you can rub around the fontanelles, the soft spots on the baby's head, and also between the eyebrows, to prevent any cradle cap. Cradle cap is a collection of dry skin layer upon layer, and often parents are too afraid to rub in the soft area of the head, thinking they may hurt the baby. Cradle cap can build up and be a thick and smelly collection of dry skin, and if your baby has a lot of hair it can take a long time to remove. So prevention is better than cure. Rub your baby's head gently in a circular motion. Then bring your baby back to the table and gently dry his hair in a circular motion. Do not put any oil on his hair or head.

Now you can undo your baby's towel and the nappy. Pick your baby up with your hand under his head. The best way to hold a baby in the bath is to gently lay him on your inner wrist with your left arm around him and your middle and index fingers gently grasping his left arm. Hold both legs and gently settle the baby into the bath, bottom first, lowering him very slowly into the bath until the water is just at his neck.

You can let the baby's legs go and let him float and enjoy the beautiful warm water, or you can put a face washer or your hand on his stomach to make him feel more secure when you put him in the bath.

Newborn babies don't need soap in their bath. They're already clean. All they need is warm water. Older babies don't need much soap either—too much soap can cause a skin reaction.

Your baby will settle down and slowly open his eyes and look around. Let him float in the water, and watch his eyes gently open as he starts to relax. There's no length of time that you need to let your baby stay in the water. If he cries in the bath, the water may be too cold or too hot. Your baby may also cry if part of his upper body is wet and exposed to the air: the bath may not be deep enough.

Keep bathing your baby if he is settled and enjoying the water. He might cry when taken out of the bath but only because he is wet. He will be very happy once he is wrapped up in a towel.

Pat your baby dry, making sure to dry under his arms and in all the creases. Two wet surfaces rubbing together can cause irritation and may lead to an infection. Lift your baby's arm up by holding his elbow. If you try and lift his arm by the hand, he will instinctively put his elbow into his body.

When he is dry, put the nappy on first. This will prevent any mess and ensure you won't have to bath him again. Put a singlet on and dress him as you desire. Wrap him up in Cath's Wrap (see page 138). Your baby is now ready for feeding.

The best advice we received from Cath was to implement a night-time routine beginning with a bath at 10 pm. No matter how unsettled Alexis had been during the day, as soon as she had her bath she was immediately calm. It was like magic. She slept through from 11 pm to 6 am from six weeks.

CHANTELLE

This process has been tried and tested by thousands of my patients and remains a successful routine for the first ten to fourteen weeks. You need to be patient and consistent, and your baby will start to sleep for four hours, then five, then six, seven and eight hours. It takes at least eight to nine weeks for a change to take effect. Patience is the first skill we as parents need to learn, and the nights you wake up to your new baby are few and don't last long, even though you feel so very tired.

When your baby is about six months old or weighs 8 to 9 kilograms, he can be bathed at 6–7 pm, wrapped, breastfed and put to bed. Every night till the baby is twelve months old, your partner can pick up the baby while he's asleep and give a bottle-feed—this is what is called a 'dream feed' or a 'rollover feed' (see page 133), and gives the baby extra kilojoules (calories) and weight gain. I would expect a baby of that age and weight to wake again at 3–4 am for a breastfeed, and then go back to sleep till 6–7 am.

> By taking the lead on night-time bathing, a bottle of formula then putting the baby to bed, my wife has been able to head to bed early to grab those few critical hours of extra sleep. It has also provided a special bonding time for me with my son. I would encourage all new fathers to seek out these one-on-one moments, as they are such special times.
>
> JULIAN

What not to do

In the early weeks there are a few things that I suggest you don't do. Don't:

- bath a newborn baby at 6 pm
- put a newborn baby to bed at 7 pm
- feed by the clock
- think that the baby has wind and is in pain if he is crying
- give the baby a dummy instead of food when he is crying
- let a baby 'cry it out'.

I parent my son Jack alone and initially I didn't think I could do Cath's 10 pm bath, bottle and bed routine, even though I wanted to. My mum suggested we make a roster for the first six weeks to help me. So between mum, my sister Marina and a few close friends a roster was made (truth was, they were all fighting over wanting to bath Jack).

It worked. I fed Jack up till 9.45 pm then handed him to whoever was on duty and went to bed. Jack was lovingly bathed every night, wrapped and given a bottle of formula. He was put to bed in the cot next to me when he was asleep. I continued to breastfeed Jack for over twelve months. If you are a single mum, get a roster going—it can be achieved.

CLARE

Cath's Wrap

When a baby is in utero he is firmly surrounded by the uterine wall, which provides resistance when he moves. The baby is born with primitive reflexes and once born needs those reflexes to be contained by the simple and ageless process of wrapping. The use of a large light wrap will keep your baby feeling safe and secure for feeding and sleeping.

Many years ago babies slept on their tummies and in fact slept very well. With the introduction of the sudden infant death syndrome (SIDS) guidelines in the early 1980s (see page 232), one recommendation was for babies to sleep on their backs. And ever since then babies have safely slept on their backs, but due to the primitive reflexes and the hand movements of newborns, this often led to unsettled babies who wouldn't sleep properly.

After many hours observing babies I invented a style of wrapping that I call 'Cath's Wrap'. My wrap allows the babies to do two very important things: one, the baby is wrapped with his hands and arms bent up (as every baby loves to sleep like this), and two, his hips and legs are flexed and capable of full movement.

Babies do not like their arms wrapped by their sides and will fight the wrap, ending up with their arms out and scratching their face. It has also been proven that it is detrimental to babies to wrap their legs straight so their hips are unable to flex.

Wrapping is the key to good feeding and sleeping. Do not use sleeping bags, just a large, soft, lightweight muslin wrap that is at least 1.2 x 1.4 metres. I wrap babies for all feeds and sleep from birth for the first six weeks of life. I continue to wrap the baby for all sleep until the baby is six months old and until the Moro or startle reflex (see page 33) has settled. Then I transfer the baby into a sleeping bag.

While wrapping a baby, there are two important factors that you must always remember.

- The baby must be able to freely move his hands under the wrap. If you have his arms wrapped down firmly by his side this will encourage the baby to fight and squirm in the wrap—no one likes to be tied and unable to move their arms.
- The baby's hips must be fully flexed. To do this you do not wrap the muslin firmly around the baby's waist and hips. You need to wrap the muslin loosely high *above* the waist and under the arms.

The startle reflex decreases as the baby gets older, and by the time your baby is six months old, it is OK to remove the wrap, as he will feel quite secure having his arms around him and his fingers in his mouth. You can start by removing one arm from the wrap, and then the other. Also, often at this time the baby starts to roll onto his tummy to sleep. This is fine, so there's no need to wrap—just put the baby to bed dressed in warm clothes with no bumpers, blankets, doonas, sheets or pillows in his cot.

We were taught to wrap with our first baby boy. It took us a little while to get its importance but by baby two and three we wrapped from day one for all feeding and sleeping. Some midwives will tell you not to wrap to feed in hospital but we found it made for a calmer, more successful feed whether my wife was breastfeeding or I was giving a bottle.

For me it was one of those jobs that I could do, and do well. When my wife was getting ready to feed I could wrap the baby and bring him to her. To this day it is probably the one thing in our household that I am the expert on, particularly for the overnight wrap. Having bub nice and snug means for a more settled sleep for everyone.

DIGBY

Playtime: Mother Nature has a plan

Babies learn by playing. They mimic us and need time to turn those observations into actions. Let your baby look around him—a tree or a shadow seen through your window will mesmerise a newborn baby.

There are many toys available for babies and shops full of specialty items that claim to help with stimulation. My suggestion is not to give babies too many toys. Simple things like the sound of your voice and movement around the house are more than enough to stimulate your baby.

Floor play

Putting babies in walkers, swings, rockers, seats or even just sitting a baby in one place interrupts Mother Nature and her developmental plan. Start putting the baby on his back and also on his tummy on a blanket on the floor, just for a few minutes in the first week between feeds during the daytime only, to help with development.

There is no need for stimulating toys to be placed over the baby, such as a baby gym with toys hanging above him. That just encourages him to lie there and stare at the swinging toys, which may startle him, rather than look inquisitively around the room and be stimulated. They love their hands, feet and toes, looking outside at the trees and shadows on the wall. Watch your baby explore his new world.

Your baby needs to be on the floor for all of his playtime. This means flat on the floor, on a clean rug—not in a seat, not in a walker, not in a swing, not in a bouncer, not in a jumper. All these 'objects' contain the baby and not only keep him in one spot, they interrupt the natural flow of his progressive natural development. Sitting the baby up in one spot is the same as using a walker or seat.

He can't explore his surroundings, learn, move, roll and progress naturally if he is attached to an object. Babies who sit too long in one spot crawl later, walk later, and their sleep is interrupted because they are not moving as much during the day. For growing babies to sleep well they need enough food (kilojoules/calories) going in, and active playtime (energy used) to achieve sleep.

Food + activity = sleep

Tummy time

Tummy time—short periods of time on the tummy—starts the first day home from hospital, especially when the baby has been fed and is content. When you have fed one side, unwrap the baby and place the baby on his tummy for a minute or two after a nappy change and in between sides *during the daytime only*.

After some time on his tummy, and once he is settled, put him on his back for a short time. Every baby is different and will tolerate floor play differently, so when your baby starts to protest and cry, that's when floor time is over. Just pick him up, wrap him and feed him again on the other side.

As he gets older, gradually increase the time your baby has on the floor.

Baby massage

During tummy time I like to encourage parents to do baby massage—*but with the baby's clothes on*. We adults like to be naked when having a massage but babies are not happy at all when cold and naked. Both you and your baby will enjoy baby massage more if you gently massage his back, legs, head and arms while he is doing tummy time, fully clothed and warm, with a full tummy. It makes sense, doesn't it!

Maternal and child health (MCH) service/community nurse

The maternal and child health nurse or community nurse plays a vital role in helping you with the baby from birth to school age. Access to these services in Australia is free and the nurses are well trained, but access will differ from state to state. It is best to contact your local council for information.

In most cases the hospital notifies the local council of the birth of the baby. In the case of home birth, the midwife at the birth will notify the council. If a baby is born before arrival to a hospital, the hospital will make the notification.

The nurse will contact you once you are home and arrange a home visit as well as follow-up visits to the local centre. The centre is a great place to meet other new mums within your area: so many friends are made for life through mothers' groups.

The nurses provide information and support to all new parents on:

- breastfeeding
- immunisation
- safe sleeping
- the weight and development of your baby
- the introduction of solids to your baby
- mothers' groups
- referrals to doctors and allied health services

- maternal health
- parenting.

There is more to feed, play, sleep

Feed, play, sleep (FPS) is taught to all new mums and dads as a way of encouraging feeding and playtime for your baby. FPS is good in theory, but in practice it is different from baby to baby. There is more to FPS than just those three simple actions; only a few babies will go to sleep after a feed, followed by a play, then another sleep. Most babies need a lot more kilojoules (calories)—milk—in their tummy and an increased amount of energy out (play) before they are capable of the magic sleep.

So it FPS fails, lots of parents are left wondering WTF (why they fail). It's not the parents' fault; it's how FPS has been communicated to the new parents. This then snowballs, leaving many new mothers feeling anxious as they try to get a baby who is crying in the cot to sleep but in reality does not want to sleep, as he is either hungry or not tired or both.

When the baby is crying in the cot after one round of feeding and play, the mother becomes anxious that her baby is not sleeping and starts trying to 'settle' him by shushing and patting. The baby's crying escalates, which sets up the new mother to think her baby is not doing what he is supposed to do.

New mums have told me they are in the baby's room doing this for up to one hour, both mother and baby ending up distressed. The mother feels there is something wrong with her milk supply, her parenting or her baby, when often what the baby needs is more time on the floor and more feeds.

Sleep will happen BUT it will be different for every baby. You have to take into account the age of the baby, the weight and the sex. Boys and girls, for example, feed, play and sleep differently.

It is impossible to prepare any new parent for sleep deprivation, by far the biggest issue I see in my consulting practice. But it is possible to solve the problem with sensible and practice advice. In my experience, gimmicky methods and fads do not work. Many books and untrained experts try to teach parenting by using different 'tricks' to get babies to sleep. Some parents with three- or four-day-old babies (still in hospital) are taught by professionals 'to hold the baby and shush into your baby's ear and this will settle them'. I can tell you without question that this is wrong.

'Sleep schools' have a waiting list as long as your arm and are geared to teach new parents how to get their baby to sleep all night. Some of the methods they teach involve patting and shushing crying babies who are far too young and too light in weight. How sad is that? That is not how we should be teaching our new, young and vulnerable parents about attachment and parenting.

Your baby is an individual

News flash: not all babies sleep all night.

He will not sleep like your friend's baby, your sister's baby, your neighbour's baby or even your other children. They are all different. Adopting a sleep routine set out in a book will not work for the majority of babies.

The newborn baby often gets days and nights mixed up in the first few weeks, and this is normal. A baby cannot sleep all day then sleep all night. They need a huge amount of feeding in the first six months to grow. I would expect a newborn baby in the first six weeks to be feeding every three to four hours during the day and at the most to sleep three to four hours after midnight.

A full daily routine is not possible until the baby weighs at least 8 to 9 kilograms or is about six months old. Daytime sleep is often two to three small sleeps of 45 minutes. They are not catnaps. They are not sleep cycles. They are normal sleeps for most babies at this age and weight.

I advise all of my new mums and dads to start my bath, bottle and bed (BBB) routine from the first day home from hospital as a first step towards getting your baby to sleep for at least three hours during the night. One of the biggest traps new parents get into is bathing a newborn baby at 6 pm. See page 129 for the full routine and how it works.

If a baby has gastric reflux he will not sleep until diagnosis and treatment are in place. Babies can be diagnosed at two to three weeks after birth. Any adult who has suffered from reflux will understand how uncomfortable the baby is, and why a baby with reflux can be labelled 'difficult' or 'unsettled'. (See page 165.)

Burping

Burping is overrated! After one breast or a bottle *gently* pat or rub your baby on his back. I prefer to hold the baby over my shoulder; that way he learns your smell by nuzzling into your neck. Don't bang his back to hopefully get the wind up; it actually comes up by itself. He is only a little baby. Be very gentle.

You do not need to pace the floor for hours burping a baby. If a baby doesn't burp the wind will pass through his gut and then come out the other end. Believe me, babies are good at wind from the other end! Don't think a baby is crying because he has wind or hasn't burped—often the baby needs more milk.

We all love to hear a baby burp since we think it confirms he had a good drink, but don't get too hung up about it. It's a normal body function and, as I say to so many new mums and dads, *if it doesn't come up it will come out*.

After babies burp they often get the hiccups. Again these are a normal body function and you can either put the baby to sleep or hold the baby or, if the baby is hungry, give him something more to drink. Hiccups, burping, passing wind, vomiting a tiny bit of milk are all normal body functions for a normal, healthy-term baby. There are more things to worry about with a baby than burps and hiccups.

Babies' nails

Everyone worries about the baby's fingernails. As previously discussed on page 33 about the Moro reflex, another reason why you should wrap your baby is to prevent him from scratching his face. Your baby's nails are really fine but they will not hurt or damage him. Mittens can be a little dangerous because a baby will instinctively put his hands into his mouth, and if he bites down on the mittens there is a chance that the mittens will go into his mouth.

I suggest you buy a soft nail file and gently file your baby's nails. A very old-fashioned way to trim nails is to bite the nails, or cut the nails with scissors. Both methods can be dangerous. Babies can get infections in their fingernails if you put their finger in your mouth or anyone else's mouth. The mouth has lots of germs and can cause what is called paronychia. I have also had people call me saying they have cut the top of the baby's finger off while trying to cut their fingernails with scissors or nail clippers. Please just get a gentle soft nail file, which will do the job.

Week 2

Feed, play and sleep routine

Bath, bottle and bed

Continue the bath at 10 pm. Your baby will be enjoying his bath more, opening his eyes and looking around while you hold him floating in the warm water. He will be so relaxed after the bath and, even though he will cry when you take him out, once he is dressed, wrapped and fed, he will settle and have a great sleep. I find it's nice to warm the towels by either placing them in the dryer for a few minutes or on a towel warmer so the baby is wrapped in a warm, snug towel. It's OK to feed the baby before the bath and also to wake him at 10 pm for the bath as the aim is to have him sleep for a long stretch of time after the bath and bottle.

Newborn babies take a lot of time and a lot of feeding, so be patient. As he grows he will be having better feeds and gaining an average of 150 grams per week. He may still only sleep for two to three hours, but be consistent and be patient. When he wakes up next is when you feed him. Always remember to talk to him, kiss and cuddle him at these special feeds—time really goes quickly, and before you know it you will have a toddler.

Daytime feeds

Often babies at this age start to wake up a bit more. So you won't have a baby who feeds and sleeps; he may have some wakeful times, sometimes for hours. There is no rule that a baby can only be awake for a certain amount of time—he is not going to get overtired, he is not going to be overstimulated. Continue to feed him, and when he is wakeful and not looking for a feed, put him on a rug on the floor and let him play.

The feeds are long and constant but remember you are giving your baby kilojoules (calories). He may require a top up of formula if you feel you are feeding non-stop. I know that top-up drinks or 'free calories' from formulas will increase his weight, decrease his crying and you will successfully breastfeed for longer. I see this with all my new mums who top up with formula and don't express. Trust me, it works.

Play

Your baby is starting to wake up and happily grasps your finger with his hand. When he is awake and looking around, don't try to rock him to sleep. Let him lie on a rug on the floor and look around at his surroundings. Talk to him, sing to him, read to him, tell him how beautiful he is. He will be startled by noises, so don't sing too loudly. You have waited nine months to hold your baby, so look at him, play gently with him, talk closely to his face. He will be able to see you and start to focus on your face.

By the end of week two . . .

- Your breasts are starting to soften up and feel more comfortable.
- An episiotomy or C-section scar will still be uncomfortable. Keep using pain relief every four to six hours as necessary.
- Blood loss should be settling down to a light brown discharge.
- Your baby is starting to have wakeful periods.
- He may be crying more, especially between 6 and 10 pm.
- Continue playtime and tummy time on the floor.
- Ring the obstetrician or hospital to make your six-week postnatal visit.
- If your partner is still at home, enjoy your time together.
- Your baby should be back to his birth weight.

Feeding chart

Date and time	Breast (mins) Left	Breast (mins) Right	Formula (mls)	Nappy Wet	Nappy Pooey	Sleep (mins)	Comments
18-Apr-16 12:41pm	3	4	180	✓	—	105	Settled easily

Feeding chart

Date and time	Breast (mins)		Formula (mls)	Nappy		Sleep (mins)	Comments
	Left	Right		Wet	Pooey		
18-Apr-16 12:41pm	3	4	180	✓	—	105	Settled easily

Feeding chart

Date and time	Breast (mins)		Formula (mls)	Nappy		Sleep (mins)	Comments
	Left	Right		Wet	Pooey		
18-Apr-16 12:41pm	3	4	180	✓	—	105	Settled easily

6

Week three

By about week three, people start asking if your baby is settling because this is what they have read or heard. Remember this is your baby and he can't be compared to other babies. All babies are different. Development takes time, and is an individual process. Some babies are very settled; others will squirm and cry. Sometimes you feel like you can't settle your baby, no matter what you do. But that's just the way some babies are born.

During the third week your blood loss will start to slow down. Everything seems to be going well and you are still on a bit of a high. Ensure you have lots of help. Enlist a friend or relative to help you with cooking, cleaning and washing so you can have some rest. We need to look after the mother in the family.

There really are no rules when it comes to caring for your baby, other than keeping your baby well fed, clean, secure, warm and loved. Some books make outrageous statements about how babies should be fed strictly by the clock and how many hours they should sleep, saying babies should only be awake for one hour at a time. Some babies can stay awake for four to five hours. A lot of the time these rules are not achievable. And if your baby does not do this, again your anxiety increases. You need to feed your baby when he needs to be fed.

Your preconceived ideas about parenting will be challenged. We all have an idea of how we want to parent. We look at other parents and think, 'I'll never do that with my baby', 'I'll never use a dummy', 'I'll never give my baby a bottle' or 'I'll never have my baby in the bed with me.'

Never say never!

You may end up doing all these things, because being a parent is hard work and you often need to do what works for your baby. You can't hurt your baby with too much love and security. You can never spoil babies with love, nor can you give them too much love.

When I had my son, I found being a new parent hard work too—and I was an experienced nurse, midwife and MCH nurse! I knew how to care for a baby but nothing could prepare me for the sleep deprivation and the 24/7 care and all the emotions that go with birth, pain, happiness, confusion, leaking full sore breasts, sore nipples, a jaundiced baby, a crying baby, anxiety, visitors, family, flowers.

But always there was the joy—oh, the joy!—of my new beautiful baby boy.

Look, watch and learn

Think of the women in Africa who have babies. They give birth, care for them, breastfeed them, keep them close—and that's it. While anxiety and parenting tend to go hand in hand, especially in the early years, these are the best years of your life, so spend them teaching and enjoying your children. Our children learn through our experiences and our words, our example, us. You are the teacher; you are the parent.

Babies do cry and I would be concerned if a baby never cried. Due to the baby being very secure in the uterus for all his pre-birth life, undressing him will make him cry, changing his nappy will make him cry, being fully naked will make him cry and taking him out of a nice warm bath will also make him cry.

Look at your baby. Often his facial expression will tell you what is wrong with him. He might make a funny face followed by a poo or a big burp.

It's important to look at your baby. *Look, watch and learn.* Your baby will tell you exactly what he's feeling. You are the parent, and know and love the baby the best.

If he is looking around, he has enough food in his tummy and is feeling very comfortable.

If the baby is squirming around and making noises, he may have some wind going around his lower bowel, which is not the end of the world or life-threatening but may cause some discomfort. Everyone has wind—it's normal for us all to pass wind, but it seems to worry new parents so much.

I receive so many calls about baby and wind, and really, this is the least of your problems, but it does cause concern for you, your family and friends. Your baby is not sick when he has wind, and often when the baby sucks either at the breast or on a bottle you may find he passes wind or has a poo. This oral/anal reflex expels what the body does not need anymore (poo) and makes more room for more food (milk) to be ingested for growth.

Your body knows what to do—trust that your baby's body does too. Mother Nature has been doing this for a long time! If a baby is sick his body will declare it: he will have a temperature or will look unwell, not feed well, be floppy, have fewer wet nappies and his poo will be different.

Feeding aversion

Feeding aversion is something not many people hear or know about. It happens when a well baby refuses the breast, bottle and/or food, and usually cries and screams when put into the feeding position. This is a behavioural response to an unpleasant or consistently stressful situation, usually feeding.

This baby usually meets his developmental milestones but is slow to gain weight and often only feeds during sleep or when really hungry. He will gain only a little weight, but continue to pass just enough urine and have an occasional bowel action.

I have seen healthy babies who are smiling one minute and as soon as you place them in the feeding position they don't just cry, they become hysterical. Then when you put them back over your shoulder, they are all smiles again. This may continue for days, even months, and lead to lifelong eating issues.

The parents will often take the baby to the MCH nurse or paediatrician, saying that the baby is crying constantly, not feeding consistently and has low weight gain. Unless the medical professionals have seen a baby with feeding aversion they can't understand what pressure the parents, especially the mother, is under, and often a baby can be diagnosed with a plethora of conditions, from reflux to the mother being diagnosed with postnatal depression.

Signs of a baby with feeding aversion

- The baby refuses to feed.
- He cries when in the feeding position.
- He closes his mouth and moves his head from side to side, refusing breast/bottle/food constantly.

- The baby drinks enough fluid to sustain fluid balance.
- He is on the third or fifth percentile for weight and has slow weight gain, or is not gaining or has static weight.
- He is meeting developmental milestones.
- He may be diagnosed and treated as a baby with reflux.

Causes

Often, feeding aversions begin early in the baby's life, because he experienced pain or trauma while being fed. These babies look and sound as if they are in intense pain when placed in a feeding position, which can be due to new mothers feeling anxious and unsupported with breastfeeding and bottle-feeding. The baby can also favour one breast and refuse the other. Others may feed for only three to five minutes before refusing the breast.

Sometimes, if a bottle is not introduced early enough (in the first few weeks of life) and the baby has to be force-fed a bottle when the mother goes back to work or is away, this can give rise to staunch refusal.

Forcing the baby to feed only makes the behaviour worse, whether it's the parents acting out of guilt, shame and anxiety, or professionals, grandparents or friends saying 'the baby will definitely take a bottle from me'.

Visits to health professionals and labelling parents 'anxious' only escalates the situation. Google and girlfriends will also offer far too much unwanted and incorrect advice.

Treatment

Don't panic. Babies are hardwired to live, not hardwired to starve. They will feed often during sleep, and a few long feeds are enough to maintain their fluid balance. Remember your baby cannot be sick and well at the same time.

If the baby stops crying once taken from the breast or bottle, he is in no pain. If the baby is in pain, he will continue to cry. If your baby is smiling and responding, he is well. Always have him checked medically to eliminate any medical disorders.

If your baby starts to fuss and wriggle at the breast or bottle (which is not uncommon after week two), take him off the breast and settle him over your shoulder, calm him and go back to basics: wrap, feed, unwrap, change nappy, rewrap, feed, cuddle and keep calm. Don't try to force him to feed.

Keep offering small frequent feeds. When the crying starts, stop feeding immediately. Be happy with small weight gains and don't compare your baby with other babies.

Ensure he has at least 3–5 wet nappies a day, depending on milk intake (breast or formula). Bowel actions will differ.

Stay home for feeds and feed in a safe and relaxing environment. A cafe or a new mothers' group is not the place for a baby with a feeding aversion.

A dummy can be helpful but remember there are no kilojoules (calories) in a dummy so don't replace food with a dummy.

Get a professional, such as an MCH nurse, to come and see how the baby reacts, cries, screams, and to watch you feeding the baby. Ask this person to try feeding the baby using a bottle.

Talk to someone if you feel anxious, depressed and angry— all perfectly normal feelings that can surface when a baby cries and refuses feeds.

Have someone you trust come and sit with the baby while you go out for a break, haircut, coffee or just a walk.

This will pass. When you are in the eye of the storm you think this will last forever. The baby will grow and get older. It does get better.

Baby Emma's story

Emma came to see me via a referral from a paediatrician. She was four weeks old, had been only gaining 30 to 50 grams per week and was on the fifth percentile for weight. She was on treatment for reflux as her mum presented to the paediatrician with a baby who would not stop crying. The paediatrician found Emma was well with no medical conditions. She was breastfed and initially took a bottle well, but her mother was advised by an MCH nurse to stop the bottle, as it would interfere with her breastfeeding. In hindsight Emma's mum wished she had continued with the bottle.

When I first met Emma she presented as a beautiful, happy and active baby. She interacted with me, gave me lots of smiles, ohhs and ahhs but as soon as I lowered her in my arms to offer her a bottle she went from a happy baby to a baby who screamed and cried for up to ten minutes before we could soothe her. It really is so sad to see such a happy and well baby go from calm to crying in seconds.

After changing her positions a few times, Emma fed on the breast and completely refused the bottle. Wrapping her for all feeds was necessary and certainly helped. We didn't offer her any bottles and exclusively breastfed her, albeit for five minutes only. But she did attach and suck. Her weight gain was slow, but she did gain weight.

Emma continued to feed well on the breast and started solids slowly. It was very hard for Emma's mum, having to constantly hold and calm her little one. It was extremely tiring and she did an amazing job, consistently responding to Emma's needs. Emma is doing well with no adverse issues due to her early feeding aversion, but it would have been so much easier without it.

Gastric reflux

Have you ever heard of, or had, heartburn? Have you ever heard of babies with such bad heartburn that they cry and cry and cry and cry? These babies are so uncomfortable, miserable and unhappy. The baby's condition can be very distressing for parents, particularly first-time mothers, who think it's their fault their baby is crying and unsettled, or their milk supply is low, or their baby has an as yet undetected allergy. The mothers don't feel confident that they're able to master the 'basic' skill of settling their own baby. These new mums tend to seek help from lactation consultants, believing that it must be a breastfeeding issue such as attachment, or not enough milk. Most commonly, it's the dreaded reflux!

A common scenario begins with the extended family (or friends), all with good intent, constantly 'advising' the new mum that her baby has 'colic' or 'bad wind'. A family member then returns from the pharmacy, having spent a lot of money on over-the-counter medicines that claim to be 'definite cures' for a crying baby with colic or wind. Unfortunately, none of these work. In fact, it gets worse unless it is treated properly by the GP or paediatrician.

Those of you who have had heartburn will confirm its constant presence. It's also very uncomfortable and you can't get rid of it. It's worse for a newborn baby. Babies can't tell you what's wrong and because they cry all the time, mothers feel inadequate, guilty and a failure.

Most people have a theory about why the baby is crying. However, the reality is that at the top of the stomach there is a sphincter that opens as the milk is swallowed and goes into the stomach. The stomach also has acid juices that are required to help break down the food to be digested. Some newborn babies have a floppy or immature sphincter and when some milk comes up, the acid in the stomach comes up too, causing burning and heartburn.

A baby with reflux struggles and fusses at the breast, arches his back and moves his head around when feeding. The mother often sees this as breast refusal. The baby cries and when he finally falls asleep and is placed in the cot, he starts crying again within five minutes, and is inconsolable until fed again. Then the process starts over.

Having a baby with reflux is very distressing for everyone: mum, dad, the extended family and, most of all, the baby. The once calm and sleeping baby has turned into a baby who will not drink well at the breast, will not sleep, cries most of the day and is very noisy overnight. The baby with reflux also loves being held upright so you find yourself walking around all day, twenty hours a day . . . a shower seems a thing of the past! The symptoms can start as early as two to three weeks after birth and can be diagnosed by your maternal and child health nurse, GP or paediatrician.

At about week three, it's possible to accurately diagnose gastric reflux. At this time, I receive phone calls from women saying, 'I can't stop my baby crying', 'I can't settle my baby', and 'He will not lie down on the floor or in the cot', 'There is something wrong with my breast milk' or 'He has such bad wind'. Look at his face—he will tell you what he is feeling.

When new mums go to mothers' group and see other babies playing happily on the floor and other mothers breast-feeding their babies with ease, it makes them feel sad, upset and even as if they are failing as a mother, since mothers of reflux babies are limited to walking around and holding their baby upright. This is so difficult for new mums.

If this is happening to you, you need to get some professional help. Gastric reflux can be treated. See a general practitioner or a specialist, and talk to them about the signs and symptoms and what treatment is available.

Common signs of reflux

- The baby is unable to lie on his back without crying.
- The baby wakes up crying.
- The baby screams suddenly and fusses at the breast or bottle.
- He is noisy overnight, gulping and squirming.
- Often a baby wakes up from a deep sleep screaming.

- After burping, the baby's face may look as if he has eaten something he doesn't like—that is because of the acid reflux from his stomach, which is sour and tastes awful.

Some babies will reflux vomit. Some do not vomit, others cough, or swallow constantly, or just cry. It's not a large amount of vomit and it's not all the milk the baby has just had, but it will be enough to make you feel concerned. Babies with reflux seem generally unhappy. However, they *are* well. Nor do they always lose weight; in fact, some actually gain a lot of weight, as feeding is a comfort for them.

Nothing quite prepares you for the realities of having your first baby. Add to that a diagnosis of reflux and you can pretty much kiss your sleep and sanity goodbye for the first few months.

Like all new mums I left hospital filled with equal parts excitement and trepidation.

'Just trust your instincts' played in my head and I thought that because I was a mum now I would instantly 'know' what my baby needed. First of many ridiculous assumptions I made as a new mum.

Over the next few weeks things began to unravel. The happy sleepy baby I brought home from hospital became increasingly unsettled. The more I fed him, the more he wanted. The more I held him, the more he wanted to be held.

'I guess this is demand feeding,' I told myself. Soon every time I put him down to sleep he would be up crying, wanting to be fed again. He was rapidly putting on weight, so everything was fine, the MCH nurse told me.

Things didn't feel fine, in fact they felt the opposite of fine. I consoled myself with the stories other mums tell each other about newborns: they cry all the time, they want to be held, they never sleep. I was a new mum, this is the gig, so I soldiered on.

By the time Cath contacted me at six weeks I was on empty. The excitement of having a newborn was gone, and my self-confidence as a mum had drained away with it. Angus cried constantly, I couldn't seem to feed him enough and/or comfort him. I had broken Google from searching. I was tired, anxious and demoralised.

Worse than something wrong with him, I was convinced there was something wrong with *me* as a mother. Everybody had advice but it was all confusing and contradictory. When Cath mentioned reflux, I was shocked. I had dismissed it because everyone said those babies vomited constantly, were underweight and fussed at the breast.

But sure enough, after three weeks on medication, Angus improved and I started to understand just how uncomfortable my little boy had been. Over time, my confidence returned. Second time around I was able to spot my little girl's reflux quickly and get help. What a different experience that was for all of us.

EMILY

Treatment

First, it's important to have reflux diagnosed by a medical professional. Your doctor will prescribe medicine and the medicine can usually take from two to seven days to work. Often an antacid is used initially in conjunction with the medicine.

Some babies need more assistance to help relieve the discomfort of reflux. The use of a thickened formula helps decrease the vomiting, thereby easing the heartburn. Also I find babies with reflux need the comfort of a dummy. The dummy must be used only after the baby has had a full feed. A baby with reflux is uncomfortable, not sick.

No medicine should be given to your baby without a physical check-up by a doctor. Often new mums think it's their fault, but it's not. The baby just needs a little bit of help to settle his tummy. He will get better, and the reflux does go away. But it is very, very hard for new parents, because you're tired and your baby is unsettled and the crying never seems to end.

Why some babies sleep well . . . and why some don't

It is no fault of any mother or father if the baby does not sleep well. Often the babies who sleep beautifully, and who are calm from day one, are just born that way. All of us have heard about babies like that, and it's hard not to take it personally when your baby is not one of the perfect sleepers, especially when you're sleep-deprived yourself.

The babies who tend to cry and squirm and fight the breast and then cry when you put them down to feed are usually suffering from gastric reflux, and that is nobody's fault. Gastric reflux can last from birth to six months and beyond in some cases. See page 165 for strategies on dealing with gastric reflux.

And there will always be those babies who, for no clear-cut reason, are simply going to find it more difficult to settle and sleep. This can be hard for parents; lack of sleep for parents over an extended period is stressful. Commencing the BBB routine from the day you bring your baby home from hospital helps (see page 129, which takes you through the BBB routine step by step).

The most difficult thing I found in the first few months was the sleep deprivation—nothing can prepare you for it! Reason and logic all go out the window when you are exhausted and it makes coping with everyday things just that little bit harder.

The best thing we did was Cath's 10 pm bath and bottle routine. I found myself sprinting to bed around 8 pm when I knew that my husband would be taking over and I could get four to five hours of precious sleep.

In the beginning it took me a while to switch off. I had to shut the door, put earphones in and listen to relaxing music, but once I did those hours of sleep helped with everything—my sanity, milk supply—and gave my husband time to be with our son. Later on down the track, we had no problems when I wanted to stop breastfeeding, as I knew he could take the bottle!

Before having kids I couldn't cope with anything less than eight hours at night. It's amazing how things quickly change, and you would give anything to have just half of that without being disturbed.

KYLIE

Routines

Days and nights can be long and isolating with a new baby, especially when your partner goes back to work. A few basics will really help:

- Have a shower and get dressed first thing every morning.
- Eat breakfast every morning and keep your fluids up.

- Limit visitors in the early days and weeks—learn to say a guilt-free 'no'.
- As you and your baby start to get some sleep, take a walk each day.
- Arrange to have coffee/lunch with a friend.

Always talk to your baby

I cannot stress enough the importance of these early days for beginning the lifetime practice of talking to your child. Don't be afraid of holding your baby and telling him what you're doing. This talk should continue for the rest of your lives, day after day, year after year, and become the 'voice' inside your child's head. It is important to pay attention to how you speak to your child, from day one. What is the voice your child is going to carry with him as he goes through life? Negative? Condescending? Critical? Angry? Or the voice of unconditional love and support, cultivating a sense of worthiness?

This is worth paying attention to. As parents we are teachers, because babies don't know what to do. We are here to teach our children what to do, how to do it, good manners, humour, fun and boundaries in life. Parents will say to me, for example, 'My baby doesn't like to be wrapped.' The baby doesn't know whether he likes to be wrapped or not. All he knows is that he needs security and we are here to teach him to be secure and be close to us as parents.

Week 3

Feed, play and sleep routine

Bath, bottle and bed

The bath routine continues. His initial birth weight and how much he is gaining each week will have an effect on his length of sleep after the bath and bottle. Hopefully your baby is starting to sleep for three to four hours after the bath. Keep doing the bath at 10 pm. I know by now the household is very tired, but the short-term pain is worth the long-term gain, and that is sleep.

If the mother is going to bed at 9.45 pm before the partner does the bath, she will be getting four to five hours' sleep at times. This will only continue to increase as the baby gains more weight and gets older.

These are the consistently hardest and longest days you will ever do as a new mum. You will be OK, you will survive and you will reflect on these days as a bit of a blur and wonder just how you managed.

Daytime feeds

Your baby really starts to wake up in week three and you may find the feeds are shorter and more efficient. This doesn't mean he isn't drinking enough but merely that your lactation is becoming more efficient and he is more wakeful, so his feeds may be frequent. But this is what he requires at this stage of his life.

Try not to problem-solve what you are doing wrong but respond to your new baby's needs by feeding him, keeping him wrapped and giving him lots and lots of cuddles and kisses. You can't spoil your baby with love.

Play

A baby at three weeks old will happily play on the floor in between feeds for up to ten to fifteen minutes during the day. This pattern of repeated feed, play, sleep will help your baby use his energy and encourage him to feed well in between playtimes.

The issue of gastric reflux will be evident during this week. A baby with gastric reflux is so unhappy when you put him down on the floor to play or back into bed. As soon as you pick him up he stops crying.

Some new parents think a baby is being 'spoiled' when, as soon as you pick him up from his cot, he stops crying. These babies are so uncomfortable from acid reflux that lying them down in bed or on a mat for a play causes the condition to worsen. Read my section on gastric reflux (see page 165) and if you think your baby may have reflux, seek medical advice.

By the end of week three . . .

- The baby may have more unsettled times. If he is squirming with discomfort, and prefers to be fed upright, ask your doctor to check for reflux.
- Your breasts start to settle.
- Any pain due to an episiotomy or C-section scar will be decreasing.
- Your partner may be back at work by now.
- You will notice your baby is starting to settle into a routine.
- At mothers' group, try not to compare your baby with others in the group.
- Weight gain continues at 150+ grams per week.

Feeding chart

Date and time	Breast (mins)		Formula (mls)	Nappy		Sleep (mins)	Comments
	Left	Right		Wet	Pooey		
18-Apr-16 12:41pm	3	4	180	✓	–	105	Settled easily

Feeding chart

Date and time	Breast (mins)		Formula (mls)	Nappy		Sleep (mins)	Comments
	Left	Right		Wet	Pooey		
18-Apr-16 12:41pm	3	4	180	✓	–	105	Settled easily

Feeding chart

Date and time	Breast (mins)		Formula (mls)	Nappy		Sleep (mins)	Comments
	Left	Right		Wet	Pooey		
18-Apr-16 12:41pm	3	4	180	✓	–	105	Settled easily

7

Week four

If this is your first baby, a lot of people will give you advice and tell you what to do and how they parent. They will relay their experiences and tell you that their way is the right way. It may well be right for their family, but that's their family, their child, not yours.

For some reason our culture has decided to tell new mothers to feed the baby then put him straight into the cot. Babies loved to be carried and be held close to you. You don't have to put your baby down in a cot during the day if you don't want to. You can cuddle your baby and hold him as much as you like. This is not going to spoil your baby; it will only help with bonding and security for the baby. This is your child. It will not set you up for 'bad habits'.

Similarly, every baby feeds in a different pattern and you will become increasingly anxious if your baby does not do what the book or your friends say. In the animal kingdom, the mothers keep their young close to them, but humans tend to put their baby into a cot by himself, leaving him alone, when all he needs is to be held or fed. The baby knows your smell and your voice.

How do you know if your baby is developing at a normal rate? Some of my most frequent consultations as a maternal and child health nurse are helping anxious mothers determine whether their baby's behaviour is normal. But when your child is a newborn, the buck stops with you. If a parent displays a particular behaviour consistently when a child is in infancy, good or bad, the baby will learn from it.

Babies at four weeks tend to start looking around and even start to try half a smile! Tummy time and back time on the floor is essential at this age, as the baby is spending more time awake, alert and looking intently at you.

This week, you'll realise that the newborn stage is passing!

Babies by two

If you have had premature twins, they will have spent their first few weeks in intensive care, and by week four you might only just be welcoming them home.

Multiple births are becoming more common for a whole host of reasons, such as IVF, and having babies after the age of 35 increases the chance of twins. Pregnancy with twins does increase the complications of pregnancy, such as diabetes, pre-eclampsia and premature birth. Pre-eclampsia is a condition particular to pregnancy that is diagnosed by: persistent high blood pressure during pregnancy or the postnatal period, evidence of protein in the urine and changes in blood platelets affecting the liver and kidneys.

Twins are hard work and I admire each and every mother and partner who has a multiple birth. It's often a long and uncomfortable pregnancy and in most cases in 2016 the babies are delivered by caesarean section. It is ideal to maintain the pregnancy for as long as possible, to prevent any issues relating to prematurity. In all pregnancies we care for pregnant women and babies and must keep in mind the health and wellbeing of both. As Emily, one of the mothers of twins I look after, said:

I spent my pregnancy worrying about a whole host of issues, very few of which pertained to actually caring for two newborns. Part of me just assumed everything would come naturally to me, part of me assumed that it couldn't really be THAT hard. People had twins every day and seemed to survive! Right?

We keep the balance of the mothers' and babies' health in the front of our minds at all times. If the mother is unwell with pre-eclampsia and having a multiple birth, for example, and the babies are well but premature, the doctor must decide whether or not to deliver the babies. The only way to 'cure' pre-eclampsia is to deliver the baby, or babies, and the placenta: the mother's body will revert to its non-pregnant state. That is why you will see babies as young as 24–25 weeks born by caesarean section in intensive care units. For Emily:

> Recovering from major surgery is no joke! In the first couple of weeks, I struggled moving around. Picking up the babies hurts, walking aches, everything seems painful. My husband is working incredibly hard to feed, change and care for the twins but it really is a two-parent job. Getting the rest I need proves difficult but gradually everything starts to ease. My wound heals well, the bleeding slows down and I'm moving around comfortably.

As I've said, twins are hard work, double the work. You have to be very organised and have not only a supportive and hands-on partner but also help at home from family, friends and, in some cases, hired help such as a nanny. It's already hard work with one baby and you have to double everything, from prams, baby capsules, cots and bassinets to nappies, wraps, bottles, formula, clothes, and the wet and pooey nappies. It's full on, so get organised by having a roster of relatives and friends to help you with changing and holding the babies.

Breastfeeding twins is definitely achievable but I strongly suggest you also give the babies formula so you can have your partner, mother, relative or friend feed one of the babies at any one time. It is virtually impossible to sleep when the twins sleep, as in the early days the babies may not sleep at the same time.

Emily and her husband Andrew have very kindly agreed to share their experience of parenting twins:

I was blindly confident about breastfeeding. Why didn't anyone warn me that it could be really, really tough! I never really entertained the idea that our babies would be formula-fed because I had just assumed that the babies would exit the womb, find their way to my nipples and gracefully attach, gazing at me lovingly as they happily guzzled.

I could not have been more wrong. The twins wouldn't attach in hospital (at all) and my milk did not come in until after we brought them home. Even then, it wasn't some wave of breast milk soaking my top like I had heard about. I never really had that 'full' feeling to start with and I panicked that I wasn't going to be able to produce enough milk.

It's important not to hurry mums who have had twins. I always reassure them that they will breastfeed and the babies will sleep and their life will settle *but* it takes time and in some cases weeks and weeks of support and guidance. The most important thing is to have the babies feed and gain weight. If the mum needs to express for a few weeks before attaching the babies to the breast, so be it.

Long-term breastfeeding is the goal. Not all babies will attach in the early days, and calm and confident care and planning is what will reassure the overwhelmed new parents.

> When we saw Cath, she showed me how to gently attach the babies and it just felt right. She was matter of fact about it and incredibly reassuring (yes, they will be able to breastfeed but you need to be patient and in the meantime, don't be afraid of formula).
>
> I was beside myself with worry and guilt and felt terrible every time we made up a bottle of formula (this was a million times a day). Gradually it did become easier but it took a lot of perseverance and patience.

I cannot stress enough: parents of twins need help, and a lot of it. If the partner can have four to five weeks off work, that is an added bonus. Remember, not only are the women looking after twins but also they are often recovering from a caesarean section, diabetes and pre-eclampsia.

In many cases twins may be born premature and the mother is often discharged earlier, leaving the babies in the special care nursery to gain weight and learn the two most basic skills of life that a new baby needs—to breathe and to suck. Once home the parents have the added responsibility of frequently visiting the new babies in the hospital and this is particularly hard on the new mother recovering from major abdominal surgery.

> We had issues with the twins needing a prescription formula due to a cow's milk protein intolerance, which also involved removing dairy and soy from my diet. They were only one week old.
>
> Cath helped me organise a new paediatrician, stool samples, kept us calm, came up with a plan and called us every single day. We had so many stupid questions and desperately needed her guidance. When there are 60 different opinions on everything and a Google search leaves you convinced you've got this whole raising babies caper wrong, it feels nice to know that you have a 'single source of truth'. We trust Cath implicitly and kept lists in our phone of questions to ask her.

I also taught Emily and Andrew Cath's Wrap (see page 138) so they could wrap the twins before feeding, and we initiated the BBB routine (see page 129). Emily could not afford the luxury of going to bed while Andrew bathed the babies . . .

it was a production line. Both parents needed to bath, dry, dress, wrap and feed the babies.

> Even though we don't leave it up to my husband to always tackle the 10 pm bedtime routine by himself it works really well for us. The babies love the bath, despite their best attempts to vomit all over their clean onesies afterwards. Gradually we notice this stretch of sleep getting a little bit longer; by about six weeks we are usually guaranteed about five hours.

It's a team effort with twins and it also depends on whether you have a boy and a girl; two boys; two girls; one baby with reflux, one without; one smaller in weight, one bigger; one active baby, one relaxed baby. Oh my, it's a full-time job and it's Groundhog Day, but there is always light at the end of the tunnel—and it's not a train!

Parents of twins are often bleary-eyed, teary and over-whelmed to the max. Parenting in the first six weeks is endless, it's emotional, it's rewarding and it's confronting. You feel guilty as all you have wanted is to have your own baby yet there are times you wish your baby would just stop crying and go to sleep so you can feel better. We *all* have times when we want to say 'Please be quiet', 'Go to sleep', 'You can't be hungry', 'What is wrong with you?' and 'I just can't do this anymore'.

For Emily:

Feed them when they are hungry, Cath tells us. If they make noise, feed them. They are so young and at this age, they just need to be fed. And don't stop feeding when they get to a certain amount. Stop when *they* are full and don't want anymore. When they cry, feed them. Wake the other twin and feed her too. Forget dragging out feed times or watching the clock. Feed them.

It sounds ridiculously simple, but it worked. In the early weeks, 99 per cent of their cries were fixed by a feed. There is nothing worse than a hungry baby's cry. To this day, I'm still unsure how new parents manage to drag out feeds or get their little babies 'into a routine' with their feeds. How on earth can you cope with that cry?

Once it sinks in that food is the only thing that will calm them, it's a relief. I'm shoving a bottle or a breast in their face every time there's a whimper. They sleep well (albeit far too briefly for our liking!) and seem so happy when they're fed. They put on weight like champions and we feel like maybe, just maybe, we're doing this right . . .

Knowing that as they get bigger they'll start to sleep for longer gives us hope and we feel positively buoyed by their gains. Healthy babies! We're succeeding at this parenting thing! Cath high-fives us after weighing Elizabeth one day and I feel triumphant.

Absolutely nothing feels good at 2 or 3 am with a baby, but there is something deep in our hearts that keeps us going as parents—we put one foot in front of the other, we fall out of bed and dribble while we feed our hungry baby at 2 am. And then, your baby smiles at you, your heart melts and the irritability of sleep deprivation disappears immediately. For Emily:

> The nights are just the worst. Being woken by those cries feels like torture. We always knew we were in for sleepless nights but we never actually understood what 'tired' feels like. Truly tired. So tired that you're worried you might drop the baby in your arms as you stumble out of the bedroom. So tired that you cry for no reason and can't seem to communicate with each other in full sentences. So tired that you feel terrified that this is the new normal—what if it's just always like this?
>
> Caring for two screaming newborns really tests our relationship. I already know how selfless my husband is but it still makes me weep when one baby cries in the middle of the night and he says, 'Don't worry, I'll get up. You sleep.' The gratitude I feel at getting a four- or five-hour stretch of sleep is insane.
>
> When we do end up with precious quiet time while the babies sleep, we're manic with indecision. Should we spend this precious half-hour eating something or having

a power nap? Can I take five minutes for a shower right now, or ever? Do you think they're about to wake up? We feel like we live our life a few hours at a time. Everything hinges on their next feed. Our priorities quickly become eat, sleep, shower. I've never shoved food in my mouth so quickly before.

The sleep deprivation messes with me. Everyone says it's the hormones but I'm pretty sure it's nothing a few good sleeps couldn't fix. I worry about everything to do with the babies and I'm convinced that when they stare at me they know I don't know what I'm doing. They know I'm just pretending.

As psychiatrist Dr Diana Korevaar, who works with a lot of mothers, said:

Women can cope with sleep deprivation much better than men. Our bodies have been changed over the course of the pregnancy and our primitive urge to get up and nurture our baby takes over our selfish wish to stay in bed. Our responsibility as a parent starts in these first six weeks, the love for our babies deepens and at some level it's the beginning of growing up.

Nowadays threat is less likely to come from our environment, in fact it is usually triggered by negative thoughts and emotions. In women, widespread change to the body and hormonal systems during pregnancy and after the birth of a baby increases the risk of anxiety and depression, and sleep deprivation, which affects most parents, also powerfully drives physiological change, which contributes to vulnerability to stress, anxiety and depression.

Whether it's parenting twins, parenting a baby alone, parenting one baby with a supportive husband and two nannies, it's still hard work and we can't escape the deep tiredness. Emily on the early days:

All we seem to do all day and night is feed, sleep, feed, sleep, feed, sleep, rinse and repeat. Then, we see glimpses of hope—they suddenly seem more alert. Xavier (the bigger twin and slightly more 'ahead' of his sister) seems to want to stay awake for a bit after a full feed. We start a 'feed, play, feed, play' cycle and it's exciting being able to interact with them; it's as if they're noticing us. They'll happily lie on the mat for a few minutes and we actually have our hands free to sip a coffee or eat something. How liberating!

I see so many women who tell me they are so tired and want to know when the sleep deprivation will finally stop. I often say 'in about twenty years', but in truth the care, the love, concern, sleep interruption never leaves you once you become a parent. And when you have twins, you have twice the load. As Emily said:

Being alone with the twins is a special kind of hell, because I find myself having to triage their cries. Other twin mums say, 'Oh, you figure stuff out' and you really do. You have to!

I try desperately to get the hang of tandem feeding and can't seem to master it, breast or bottle. In a pinch though, I can feed them both in their bouncers or propped up on a twin-feeding pillow. I become a pro at feeding one and rocking the other one's bouncer with my foot. I'm constantly talking to the other twin, begging them to be patient while I feed their brother or sister, thanking my lucky stars that surely this means our babies will grow to be patient adults. They have no choice.

I worry about them developing a complex about being neglected. When I'm feeding one and the other one screams at me, I feel like the worst mother in the world. I can't physically pick up and tend to both babies at once so it's basically choosing the one who screams the loudest. Cath says we have to 'learn to like their cry'. When my husband goes back to work and I'm with them all day, it is just non-stop juggling them for hours on end—feeding one, quickly moving to the next, trying to take the 'edge' off them so I can go back to the first twin, and so on and so on until they're both content and happy.

Emily went on to fully breastfeed her twins, giving them one bottle of formula initially after the bath and now as a dream feed. The twins sleep well, play and are happy babies but the work, the hard work, still continues for Emily and Andrew.

The growing baby

Your newborn baby is growing up. Where he once fed and slept, fed and slept, he now spends more time awake—you have a baby who is social, who wants to learn, play and interact.

He wants to talk to you. He wants to look at his hands, smile and wave his arms. He will delight in making noises that you do not understand, but it all sounds great. He is learning to communicate.

When the baby has had enough of anything, he will let you know. If he's on the floor, he will start protesting. Once playtime is over, pick up your baby, change his nappy, rewrap him and offer the other breast. You can keep doing this until he needs to go to sleep. Your baby will sleep when he is tired and needs to sleep, not when *you* want him to sleep.

You might like to keep a diary of all your baby's new tricks. When your baby is a teenager, show him the diary of what happened when he was a baby—he will love reading about it. Film your baby and take lots of photos—you can never have too many photos! As adults we love to see ourselves as babies.

The first six weeks really are a blur. I read a lot about labour and breastfeeding and the demands of a newborn, but until it became a reality none of it really made sense. I learnt very quickly that the 'must have' devices/toys/things that people insist you need for a baby are just nonsense.

As Cath taught me, the most important thing in the first six weeks is to feed and wrap. Getting back to basics was the best thing I could have done. It can be quite overwhelming when you are experiencing a newborn for the first time and EVERYONE is giving you his or her opinion on what you should do.

Ignoring all the chatter and just concentrating on feeding my baby and wrapping was the advice that stood out to me. Not trying to problem-solve why he slept for four hours one day and two hours the next, and just thinking that it will change tomorrow and that's OK, helped me with the first six weeks.

Enjoy the moment, feed whenever, wrap and sleep when you can.

BRYDIE

Normal development

Let your baby develop in his own way. Mother Nature has a plan. She knows we have an innate process in our bodies to develop. Giving a baby too many toys or putting a baby in a walker, swing or a jumper will only interrupt Mother Nature's natural process of development. Let nature take its course.

Babies all over the world develop the same way. We don't need to interfere. Don't compare your baby with others. Some babies roll early. Some babies talk early. Some babies talk late. Some babies walk late. Some babies are born with teeth. Some babies don't get teeth until ten months. It's all normal.

A baby needs around 1000 hours of floor time before walking.

Normal development throws some strange situations at you. Once babies roll and start moving on the floor, they will move backwards before they crawl forwards. Don't ask me why, but they all do it—and don't be surprised if you find your baby under the couch!

A baby needs to crawl first, and then be capable of sitting himself. He will commando-crawl with his tummy on the floor and then get up on all fours and rock. Get ready and child-proof your home as they will be taking off soon!

Crawling on hands and knees is important for many levels of development. Crawling plays a major role in the development of an infant's strength, balance, spinal alignment, visual-spatial skills and socioemotional development.

Finally, the baby will pull himself up and cruise around the furniture, holding on for dear life. When a baby is ready to walk, he will stand alone, legs apart and hands held high. It's a picture of balance—Mother Nature again in all her glory! Then, when ready, a baby will take his first steps. A few tentative steps at first, then plop onto the floor. With balance and courage, off he goes . . . running!

Babies need food, love and warmth. Beyond that, they don't need too many shiny, jingle-jangle toys. The less they have, the more they'll explore the world and themselves. The toy gyms that sit over babies keep them lying on their backs, staring at the toys, which can result in the babies having flat heads and slower than normal development.

Once you take the toy gym away from the baby you will find that he will start to move in a circle on his back, reach out to touch other things, look at his hands, then start to reach over and eventually roll.

The same applies to sitting your baby in one spot. They will happily sit there all day without much movement. Often these babies tend to miss the hands and knees crawling stage and end up doing a bum-shuffle crawl.

Your baby needs to crawl on his hands and knees, and the only way he can do that is to gain strength through his body so he can support himself off the ground. He also needs head control, which is gained through tummy time and rolling. There is no need to hurry or make your baby crawl. You cannot force this process other than leaving him free to roll, and gain strength in his arms and upper body. The natural process of balance is developed by the brain, which will make it possible for the baby to coordinate essential arm and leg movement.

Your baby needs to learn how to sit by himself, which happens after he is crawling and can move himself into the sitting position. If this process is missed the baby will just sit and sit when what he needs to do is crawl, crawl, crawl so he can learn how to stand, cruise around the furniture, stand alone and then walk. Get ready, because running comes soon after.

Hand-and-knee crawling is really important for spatial awareness and learning how the three-dimensional world works. It also helps his eyes deal with depth and distance. The cross movement of arms and legs through crawling on the floor is often preceded by a tummy drag or commando crawl.

When you're with your baby, look at his face. Talk to his face and tell him how much you love him. Say his name with the same intonation that you would use with anyone else. Your baby can hear you and he loves watching your face. You are food, love and warmth to your baby.

Parenting can be challenging, but it can also provide a turning point, a threshold beyond which we can choose to be fully present for whatever each new day brings with curiosity and an open mind.

Parenting provides us with an opportunity to shape our own personal development according to what we most want to bring to the precious experience of parenting a child.

Fourteen items a baby doesn't need

- A swing: babies do not need swings, they need the floor!
- A bouncer: again, the floor is the safest and most practical place for the baby.
- A walker: babies will walk when they are developmentally ready. Walkers are dangerous.
- Seats: babies do not need seats, they do not need to sit up until they can crawl. They need to play on the floor.
- Bath seats: babies need to relax and float in the bath.
- Necklaces: they will not help your baby with teething and can be a choking risk if they break.
- White noise: they do not need white noise to sleep.
- An egg-shaped thermometer that displays the temperature in the baby's room, changing colour according to whether it's warm, hot or cold.
- An ear thermometer: you will know when your baby is so hot and sick. A digital thermometer is better.
- Shoes: not until the baby is walking and running around the house!
- A gourmet food menu: a baby needs clean and plain food.
- Play gyms: they keep the baby still and staring at the toys rather than looking around the room.
- Bumpers and toys in the cot: not advised for SIDS.
- Muslin wraps over the prams: fresh air is good and the baby loves to look at the world around him.

Week 4

Feed, play and sleep routine

Bath, bottle and bed

Like Groundhog Day, the bath, bottle and bed routine continues each and every night at 10 pm. The baby will be more settled, enjoying his bath and taking more of his bottle. As the weeks go by the volume of the bottle will increase. I always offer babies more in the bottle than required. This allows them to have enough milk as they will stop when they are full. You cannot overfeed a baby, and all babies will take a different amount of formula after the bath.

Daytime feeds

Daytime feeds will continue to be efficient and consistent. The baby will often have three-hourly feeds in the morning and will demand more as the day continues. Babies often feed continuously from 6 pm, commonly known as the witching hour. Continue to feed him, so he gains weight, and also ensure he has lots of playtime on the floor to use his energy. Remember: Food + activity = sleep. At the four-week check from your MCH nurse you will see an increase in weight. This always makes you feel positive.

Play

Playtime and tummy time are the key to your day. He will be able to move his head from side to side and you will be surprised how strong his neck is becoming. Tummy time is necessary at least six times a day between feeds. He only needs to do it for a few minutes at a time, but it will enable him to be strong and happily play on his tummy.

You don't need to stay home—put the baby in the pram and go for a walk so he can play in the pram. He will shut his eyes to bright light so there is no need to cover the pram with a wrap; let him look around and breathe in the fresh air. He will watch your face with great interest, especially when you feed and talk to him. He will follow you with his eyes when you hold him close to you. Your baby is waking up.

By the end of week four . . .

- You may have attended a new mothers' group.
- The baby will start to put on weight steadily now.
- You can manage a walk confidently.
- You may be able to drive if you have a C-section (check with your obstetrician).
- The BBB routine is now doing very well and your baby may sleep a good four hours after the bath.

Feeding chart

Date and time	Breast (mins)		Formula (mls)	Nappy		Sleep (mins)	Comments
	Left	Right		Wet	Pooey		
18-Apr-16 12:41pm	3	4	180	✓	—	105	Settled easily

Feeding chart

Date and time	Breast (mins)		Formula (mls)	Nappy		Sleep (mins)	Comments
	Left	Right		Wet	Pooey		
18-Apr-16 12:41pm	3	4	180	✓	—	105	Settled easily

Feeding chart

Date and time	Breast (mins) Left	Right	Formula (mls)	Nappy Wet	Pooey	Sleep (mins)	Comments
18-Apr-16 12:41pm	3	4	180	✓	–	105	Settled easily

8

Week five

You've made week five!

Feel proud of yourself. Your baby is starting to look around him, and those smiles he gives you are not wind—he knows you. He knows your smell. He knows your voice. He knows your touch. After someone else holds your baby, he will come back to you and snuggle into you. Your presence calms him. It's the best feeling.

The ongoing routine

Remember: food, love, warmth.

You're still feeding, loving and wrapping your baby. If you've kept the routine of the bath that you established early on, you might find your baby now wants to go to bed earlier. He may have a bath at 9.30 pm, have a feed and go to bed. He may even be sleeping longer.

Weight gain is increasing and the time it takes to feed your baby may be decreasing. Your baby may only suck for five to ten minutes, compared to those long feeds you did when he was a newborn. Your lactation is becoming established, and your baby is now efficient at feeding and your breasts feel soft again.

You may find at some stage during the day that your baby has long feeds, while at other times, little feeds. Every feed is important. Trust your baby. He knows how much he wants.

In the mornings when you wake, it's a good routine to feed your baby while he is wrapped up. Then, after the feed, unwrap him, change his nappy and put him on the floor to have some time moving and kicking. You don't need to put the baby back to bed after every feed. It's a common practice that a lot of mums fall into. They feed the baby and put him back into the cot. Then, ten minutes later, the baby is awake.

Your baby doesn't want to sleep all the time because he is busy learning. So feed your baby, put him on the floor and let him have some physical exercise. Tummy time is especially important because it strengthens his neck and back.

Attachment

Attachment between mother and baby, and between father and baby, begins in utero. Once the baby is born, even though exhausted from labour, the mother attaches by looking, touching and smelling her new baby. The baby attaches by sucking, hearing, smelling and touching the mother.

The attachment between mother and baby within the first twelve months is so important. I often refer to the emotional wet cement that babies are in when born and how, as parents, it is up to us to mould how the baby thinks, reacts, attaches, bonds and loves. Emotional and physical attachment is as important as nutrition and housing for the baby and his physical survival.

Ten ways to help attachment

- Holding and cuddling your baby.
- Kissing and holding your baby close.
- Responding to your baby's needs when he cries and needs your contact.
- Looking at your baby's face and having eye contact.
- Getting to know how he responds to you, your tone of voice, your smile, your singing.
- Playing with your baby. Play is how children learn adult practices and this play starts at birth and continues through childhood, teenager and adult life.
- When talking to your baby, tell him how lovely he is.

- Ask him if he is going to give you a smile, and praise him when he does.
- Talk to him in the bath, make it enjoyable.
- Remember your words become his inner voice for life.

How we are taught to love in life depends on our own parenting. Our parents' voices in our heads become the way we think and learn, and in turn how we treat others. Our emotional security as adults depends on our early years of love, connection and attachment through our parents. Children who display behavioural problems at school learnt those behaviours at home, during their early years.

I don't mean 'attachment parenting'—constant carrying, extended breastfeeding, co-sleeping and minimal separation of mother and child—but more the positive, gentle and consistent parenting of a baby from day one. To achieve attachment you don't have to sleep with your baby 24 hours a day or breastfeed for years, but as the years pass the babies develop a strong and trusting relationship that is built on love and security.

Babies should not be fearful of their parents or have to gain their love, trust and security. In turn parents need not feel abnormal if they hold the baby for an extended time, respond quickly to the baby's needs and talk in a positive, loving voice.

I encourage you to talk to your baby from day one in a positive and loving way. Explain who you are and tell him how much you love him. Tell him everything. Hold him close, look him in the eye, sing, say lots of words, offer lots of love. Then when the emotional cement eventually sets, that little person you loved and cared for so positively and deeply will in turn become a loving and caring person.

Children learn love, empathy and understanding from us as parents. If we show this by example during the early years, it enhances their capacity to love and show empathy and understand others. Children are not bad and are not naughty or destructive—that is learnt behaviour from adults while that emotional wet cement is being moulded.

As new parents you will be constantly told not to hold your baby as 'you will spoil him'. You cannot spoil your baby with too much love. I am asked daily by new parents, as I encourage them to hold their baby after feeds for hours sometimes, 'Won't we be making a rod for our backs and spoiling him if we just hold him?'

It seriously breaks my heart when I hear this as young people are already thinking it's normal to feed and put a baby down in a cot alone and crying, so they can 'self-settle'.

I can remember being at a barbecue with my son, who was about three months old. One man said to me, 'Is that kid velcroed to you? You are always holding him.'

I can remember saying to this man that I *enjoy* holding my son, and he was happy in my arms, so what really was the problem? He replied that I was spoiling him.

Some books and sleeping programs encourage new parents to have no eye contact with the baby, especially overnight, as this may encourage stimulation.

I encourage you to make the night feeds loving. Talk gently to your baby and make eye contact. These days will seem long, but they are few and they go very quickly.

The detachment of babies from the outside world and stimulation is evident on our streets every single day.

Look around at new mothers walking their babies, trying desperately to get them to sleep, their prams covered by blankets or muslin wraps so the baby does not get stimulated. Please take the blankets and wraps off the prams. The babies need the sunshine and fresh air. Your baby will naturally fall asleep just looking at the trees, the clouds and other people, and hearing the birds. But most of all, he can see your face, so look, talk and smile at your baby. If he is tired, your baby will sleep in the pram while you are walking—without a cover.

Attachment takes place not only through breastfeeding; the attachment is as strong for women who bottle-feed their babies. The most important thing is a happy mother; that is what drives the attachment and creates a lifelong bond of love and security between mother and child.

Your emotions

Having a baby is hard work. You're sleep-deprived and you will cry, sometimes at silly things. Your hormones are all over the place, and crying is very normal.

The baby blues usually happen around day two to three and believe me, you will cry at anything good, bad, sad or happy. You feel irrational and out of control and you just cannot stop the tears from pouring out. This is the day for no visitors. The baby blues usually last a day or two, and no other treatment is required other than lots of TLC, support and understanding.

My good friend and colleague Dr Diana Korevaar, who currently works as a psychiatrist specialising in the areas of women's mental health, pregnancy and perinatal psychiatric disorders, has kindly written the information below about the psychological impact of pregnancy, childbirth and parenting on new parents.

Life as a new parent

While the risk of depression and anxiety increases during pregnancy and in mothers and fathers of young babies, modern psychological methods generally provide very effective treatment when help is sought early. Signs to look out for include difficulty sleeping, increased irritability, lowered mood and an inability to think clearly.

Modern psychological techniques, in particular mindfulness, which is drawn originally from the contemplative tradition of Buddhism, take advantage of the process of neuroplasticity and have the potential to transform life's challenges into opportunities to build emotional resilience and to strengthen relationships. Mindfulness techniques are sophisticated skills that help to ground us in the present moment, regulate powerful emotions and interpret more accurately what is going on around us and within our own minds.

When applied to the task of parenting, mindfulness can help us interpret with more accuracy the behaviour of our baby or child. We become less vulnerable to self-doubt and unhelpful patterns of thinking and are more able to skilfully navigate feelings of ambivalence, irritability or even anger without automatically blaming others or ourselves.

Occasionally in the treatment of perinatal depression or anxiety, medication may be recommended to augment psychological techniques. When chosen carefully, it can significantly improve brain function, allowing recovery to occur and psychological methods to be used more effectively. The prospect of medication use can cause anxiety for some parents, but research suggests that the emotional wellbeing of parents is of the utmost importance to the healthy development of children.

DR DIANA KOREVAAR

If you continue crying, if you feel anxious, worried or scared and have feelings that you might harm yourself or your baby, please get help. There is a lot of help available for women who feel very anxious after birth. See 'Seeking help' on page 271 for a list of resources.

> I can remember looking at my baby and thinking he is adorable but I wasn't in love with him straightaway. My partner was, and I envied his love and connection. I cared for and fed my baby but it wasn't until he was about five to six weeks old that I got that glorious feeling. I felt guilty and disconnected for not loving him at birth.
>
> EMMA

During antenatal care most women are not asked if they have any family history or personal history of anxiety and/or depression. Studies show that women who are treated in the antenatal period for anxiety and/or depression have a reduced risk of having postnatal depression.

Often women who have had anxiety and depression before pregnancy believe it is better for them and their growing baby to be off antidepressant medication. The opposite is correct. We now know that women who have a past history of anxiety and/or depression and stay on their medication, managed properly by a GP or psychiatrist along with their obstetrician and/or midwife, maintain stability during their pregnancy and in their postnatal period.

As part of working in Dr Len Kliman's rooms I consult with most women prenatally. If there has been previous anxiety and/or depression, we can arrange for the patient to be seen during the antenatal period by a specialist psychiatrist and/or psychologist if necessary.

Often within the antenatal period emphasis is on the physical health and growth of the mother and baby, and not the psychological side of the pregnant mother. During the antenatal period psychological issues are rarely discussed and many women will not divulge their past or family history.

For some women, because of hormonal changes and fear of childbirth, anxiety and depression can increase during this period. If you are pregnant and have a history of anxiety and depression, talk to someone—your GP, midwife or obstetrician. It will make you feel more in control and less anxious. Research indicates that up to one in ten women have antenatal anxiety and depression.

Many women have experienced anxiety to a degree, but if it becomes a daily occurrence and you feel constantly anxious during your pregnancy, or tearful, irritable or sensitive, again, talk to your GP, midwife and/or obstetrician. If you have extreme fears, especially about the upcoming birth, it is best to talk to your obstetrician or midwife, as meditation and mindfulness training can be extremely helpful during this period. What we don't want is this anxiety to follow on to the postnatal period, when sleep deprivation is added to your already anxious state, plus the care of a baby that can become overwhelming at times.

We now know that identifying and managing stress in pregnant women and new parents is incredibly important. Research has shown us that the children of parents who are emotionally resilient tend to do better in life generally. They are able to learn more effectively, have more stable relationships and are less likely to suffer from anxiety and depression themselves later in life.

Research into emotion and the neurobiology of relationships has opened our eyes to the vast complexity and importance of the relationships we have with those around us. Within hours of birth babies have the capacity to be soothed and calmed by a carer who can connect with them emotionally, attune to their distress, and respond wisely and calmly.

While it is normal for babies to respond to discomfort such as hunger, tiredness or pain by crying, deep within the brain of a parent there can be strong and subconscious reactions, which contribute to the stress process. As adults, when we feel stressed a common response is to get into problem-solving mode. However, when we get caught up in our own heads—thinking, planning and searching for causes of why our baby might be crying—an emotional disconnection occurs which can impair our capacity to accurately interpret what is happening and respond wisely.

DR DIANA KOREVAAR

Medication for anxiety and/or depression plays an important role in the wellbeing of the mother, baby and family. It can be used safely during your pregnancy and postnatally while you breastfeed. I say to worried patients who are concerned about taking medication that, if they had pneumonia and required antibiotics to get well, they would have no hesitation in taking them. You need to think of antidepressants in the same way: some women have a chemical imbalance that requires medication.

The symptoms of anxiety and depression are the same as you would experience before pregnancy, with the added bonus of hormones, sleep deprivation during the antenatal period, discomfort from pelvic pain, heartburn and other pregnancy side-effects. You may feel sad, unmotivated, guilty, hopeless, inadequate, irritable and an overwhelming sense of anxiety about the upcoming labour and responsibility of parenting. Please talk to your GP, obstetrician and/or midwife.

Anxiety and depression affect not only women but men too. During the pregnancy and postnatal period your partner may feel as sad and inadequate, and anxious, about the responsibility of parenting as you do. There is fabulous medical, psychiatric and psychological assistance available. You are not alone: help or a consultation with someone you trust is only a phone call away.

Having help during your antenatal and postnatal period has such a profound effect on your parenting: you are doing the right thing not only for yourself but also your baby. At the end of this book are phone numbers and websites that can help you (see 'Seeking help' on page 271).

Over the last few decades, the management of stress and psychological disorders such as anxiety and depression has been fundamentally transformed by scientific research into a process called neuroplasticity, which is the process by which brain cells are constantly establishing new connections with each other. The brain quite literally reshapes itself, reinforcing patterns based upon our thinking, emotions and our behaviour. What this means is that the more time we spend feeling anxious, irritable or frustrated, the more likely it is that these will be the emotions that arise when we feel challenged.

The human brain operates like a simulator that is constantly turned on, and most of the time we live life on automatic pilot. We may be sitting quietly having our morning coffee, feeding a child or driving the car, but typically we are not fully present to that experience. Our mind is constantly moving; perhaps rehearsing a conversation with a partner, responding to a text message or thinking about what we might have for dinner. As we are doing this, our brain and body respond as if the simulation was really happening. Whenever the content of our thinking and planning is even mildly negative, cascades of stress-related hormones and neurotransmitters are released and bath the cells of our nervous system, gut and heart.

Humans are primarily social creatures, and research has shown how the structure and function of our brains are affected by the emotions, tone of voice and facial expressions of others in a way that is largely beneath conscious awareness. When we are with a person who is angry or irritable, we are more likely to feel tense or in some way not safe. On the other hand, when we are in the company of someone who is calm and in good spirits, this too influences our emotional state, due to an impact upon hormonal systems and neuroplasticity. If we are to do parenting well, we need to be proactive about emotional wellbeing and healthy relationships.

DR DIANA KOREVAAR

Week 5

Feed, play and sleep routine

Bath, bottle and bed

There is no change in the bath, bottle and bed routine. Hopefully the mother is getting more than five hours' sleep if she goes to bed before the baby's bath and the baby wakes up around 3 am. The volume of the bottle will continue to increase even by 5–10 mls each week. Don't stop giving the bottle as the baby will never refuse the breast, but if he stops having the bottle he will not take it again.

Daytime feeds

Daytime feeds are still reactive. Gone are the days of feeding your baby every three hours. He will need to feed in response to his play and tummy time (see page 143). His feeds will be more demanding as the day goes by and your breasts may feel softer and not as full. Your breasts are fuller in the mornings and, as you go about your day, you do feel depleted but remember your lactation is a given—it doesn't just go away, and pumping or taking medications does NOT increase your milk supply. If your baby is requiring lots of feeding, make life easier for yourself—top him up with formula. Sometimes there are no alternatives and at the end of the day your baby needs food to grow, develop and sleep.

Play

Playtime is getting a bit more interactive now and your baby is capable of enjoying time on his tummy on the floor. He doesn't need toys dangling over him on a play gym, he has the perfect toys attached to him already—his hands. It's really important to let him be on his back and his tummy in between feeds to use up his energy and to be stimulated by his surroundings. If you have a window, lay him safely near the window (not in direct sunlight). He will love watching the trees, shadows and life outside his home.

By the end of week five . . .

- Your routine is going really well.
- Blood loss has usually settled down completely.
- Your breasts have settled too.
- The baby is starting to look around.
- Playtime on the floor is increasing.
- You should be pain-free.

Feeding chart

Date and time	Breast (mins)		Formula (mls)	Nappy		Sleep (mins)	Comments
	Left	Right		Wet	Pooey		
18-Apr-16 12:41pm	3	4	180	✓	—	105	Settled easily

Feeding chart

Date and time	Breast (mins)		Formula (mls)	Nappy		Sleep (mins)	Comments
	Left	Right		Wet	Pooey		
18-Apr-16 12:41pm	3	4	180	✓	—	105	Settled easily

Feeding chart

Date and time	Breast (mins)		Formula (mls)	Nappy		Sleep (mins)	Comments
	Left	Right		Wet	Pooey		
18-Apr-16 12:41pm	3	4	180	✓	—	105	Settled easily

9

Week six

You've made six weeks! I feel I've gone on the journey with you. I celebrate the six-week milestone with many parents. I see them come for their check-up with a new confidence and a new story. They've survived the first six weeks, and many women feel sad leaving our care after the six-week appointment, as such a great bond is built during the pregnancy.

You can't explain to anyone how you felt, managed or coped during those first six weeks, but when you reach that milestone you feel fantastic. It's the love, the sleep deprivation, the smiles, the poo-filled nappies, the vomit, the crying. It's your tears. It's the love for a newborn baby.

Breastfeeding is now a lot easier. You might still want to top up with some formula and that's OK too. Think back to that day when your baby was born, when you had no idea what you were doing. Six weeks down the track, you feel a lot more comfortable. There will be some hurdles ahead, but you'll get over them.

Spoil yourself

You need to have some physical distance from your baby, especially in the early days. It's very hard when you have a baby at your breast, feeding all the time. There's crying and nappy changes, not to mention the lack of sleep. And you're it. You are number one, you're in charge.

So have a date night every now and then. Go out one night for a quick meal or to the movies. Have someone you know and trust look after the baby. It's amazing how well you'll feel coming back. Believe me, all you will do is talk about how advanced, adorable and fabulous your baby is compared to other babies!

How grandparents love

Once you have given birth grandparents can play an amazing role in your life and also within society, often caring for children once new mums and dads go back to work. I could not have survived the early years without the love and support of my mum and dad. My son Lachlan still remembers his Nan and Pop taking him for walks to the park, waving to the train drivers on the way, walking along the beaches of

Sandringham, and his Pa taking him on train and tram rides. These are the special, lifelong relationships and memories that grandparents build with your child.

Not only will having your parents and/or your parents-in-law around help you understand and respect what they have done for you and your partner, but also you may be amazed by their unconditional love and their ability to multitask by keeping you all fed, the house clean and the washing done.

I talk to so many new grandparents and often they sit silently in my room as I help the new mother with feeding and parenting. It doesn't take long for the grandmother to feel relaxed and confident enough to say, 'That's exactly how we did it.' Often new mums think their mums are not up with the new ideas, but do listen to your mum—she is usually right!

You need a lot of help and support in the first six weeks and it usually comes from your parents or your partners' parents.

How to manage family helpers

- Have a roster so you don't have everyone in your home at the same time.
- Write a list of chores for your relatives.
- Explain the SIDS guidelines to your family as sleeping positions have changed, but your parents may say, 'Well, I did that with you and you survived.' You did, but many

babies didn't, so give them some written information to help them understand.

- Use the time with your mum or mother-in-law to ask them to do specific tasks.
- Have a shower or nap while they are there so they can hold the baby.
- Ask them to answer the phone or door so you are not telling your birth story 30 times a day.
- Explain your approach to parenting.
- If parents are coming from overseas or interstate, organise a place nearby for them to stay. Everyone will feel happier and relieved.
- If any family members are smokers explain about no smoking in the home or around the baby and the risks associated with smoking.
- Advise your parents to be immunised against whooping cough.

Being a grandparent is an unexpected pleasure to your parents, who are often eager to help and may worry constantly about you. You were the baby in their arms not long ago, and all they want to do is help.

If you don't have a very good relationship with your mum and/or your mother-in-law, I'm sure they will still want to help you.

I remember doing a home visit and the daughter was in her bedroom in tears, annoyed with her mother as she wasn't helping her much with the new baby. The new grandmother just wanted to help but didn't 'want to interfere'. I was caught in between the two! I encouraged the new mum to write a list of things she would love her mum to do, gave them both some structure, and life moved on; both women were happier and their tempers settled.

Lots of new mums have parents and parents-in-law living overseas, and having them staying with them in their house after the baby is born can cause some tension. Everyone is tired and needs some space and respect.

Today I accompanied my only daughter Sarah to Len Kliman's rooms, for a pre-arranged appointment to seek your help.

First-time mother Sarah was feeling extremely low, and you gave her back her confidence and strength to keep formula-feeding, toss the breast pump, and keep offering her breast to her daughter Stevie. We were so pleased for her that Stevie had put on weight today, and you reinforced all the sensible commonsense breastfeeding techniques that would help her.

Living 230 kilometres from Melbourne, the best I can do is come to Melbourne weekly and I was very pleased to meet you today and hear your experience. I hope now Sarah will relax and Stevie will thrive.

Thank you, thank you.

ONE VERY APPRECIATIVE GRANDMOTHER, SANDRA

Ten ways new grandparents can help

- Cook lots of food for the freezer.
- Plan a roster with the new family that suits them.
- Assist with the laundry and cleaning the house.
- Communicate with the other new grandparents so there is no competition.
- Be flexible and go with the flow.
- Be careful about offering advice (even though you have raised healthy children yourself).
- Take a deep breath if you don't like the new baby's name or the way it's spelt. It really will grow on you in time.
- Be a grandparent—this baby is not yours. It is very hard to stand back and not say 'I did it this way'.
- Remember everyone is tired and emotional and the new parents will be amazed by everything the new baby does. Be patient and enjoy every day.
- Take the new baby for a walk with the new mum to give her some confidence.

Cultural confinement

Some cultures practise cultural confinement, where the new mother and baby stay indoors at home for 40 days and do not receive visitors. This traditional postnatal practice helps the new mum recover from pregnancy, labour and childbirth, while the mother or the mother-in-law cares for her and her baby. Most community health services offer home visits to families practising cultural confinement. All communities have their own confinement practices, special traditions and foods that are given to the new mother.

Your changing baby

You'll see an incredible difference in your baby within six weeks. If you compare photos from birth, you will see how your baby has developed. His head has grown, he's longer and he's put on weight. Your baby will turn his head to follow noises, smile at you and be quite interactive. You'll talk to each other, not really understanding, but still communicating. He's learning from your every word, every movement. You are the teacher. You are his life. You are his food, love and warmth.

By six weeks you need to think about how you're feeling emotionally. If you are crying continuously, having negative thoughts or you're finding it very tough being a mum, get some help. There are some wonderful practitioners around who can help you. If you're crying, it's not always postnatal depression. Some of us just need to have a cry every now and then. You're tired, emotional and busy.

If it's more than crying, if you're having negative thoughts and not feeling happy as a mum, please talk to someone. Talk to your partner, a professional or a friend. There is a lot of help and a lot of understanding about anxiety and depression within the community.

The six-week check-up

At six weeks, it's great for you and your baby to have a check-up with your obstetrician. It's just so wonderful to be a parent of a six-week-old baby. Your baby is feeding, you feel a lot more settled, and when you see pregnant ladies you look at them and think, 'Oh my, you have a journey ahead of you.'

The postnatal visit to your obstetrician or midwife usually consists of assessing how you are feeling, making sure that your uterus is back into shape, that you're breastfeeding OK and feeling all right with parenting. The doctor will also check that your wound has healed, whether it is vaginal or from your caesarean section.

You will also discuss contraception, even though that may be the last thing on your mind! Resume sexual relations with your partner whenever you feel comfortable and ready.

If your baby saw a paediatrician after the birth, a six-week check-up is usual. The doctor will make sure your baby is doing well and perform a full check from head to toe.

If you ever have concerns about your baby, please seek advice. Trust your gut feeling. In most communities there are nurses who help you with education and the development and progress of your baby. Having your baby weighed and measured is reassuring for the parents, and often a bragging right. Keep in contact with your community nurse.

Immunisation

Immunisation may start at six or eight weeks. This is controversial for some people. We are a small world now. Every day, people travel all over the world, and there are many diseases around. For this reason, we need to immunise and protect our babies.

I encourage you to read up on immunisation and talk to professionals about it. I am in favour of immunisation for all children and adults. Unfortunately lives have been lost because people refuse to immunise their children.

As the Australian Department of Health says: 'Immunisation is the most significant public health intervention in the last 200 years, providing a safe and efficient way to prevent the spread of many diseases that cause hospitalisation, serious ongoing health conditions and sometimes death.' Since the introduction of vaccinations for children in Australia in 1932, deaths from vaccine-preventable diseases have fallen by 99 per cent. Immunisation programs prevent about three million deaths each year.

For immunisation to provide the greatest benefit, a sufficient number of people need to be vaccinated to halt the spread of bacteria and viruses that cause disease—a phenomenon called 'herd immunity'. The proportion of the population that has to be immune to interrupt disease transmission differs for each vaccine-preventable disease, but for most diseases it is around 90 per cent. For a highly infectious disease such as measles, this is up to 95 per cent of the population.

Immunisation uses the body's natural immune response to build resistance to specific viral infections, but without the person suffering the symptoms of the disease.

SIDS

We all worry about our children. We think once the baby is born the worry is over. But the worry has just begun.

Cot death or sudden infant death syndrome (SIDS) is still a concern in our society, despite a reduction in the number of deaths. There are many factors that can reduce the chance of SIDS.

You should always put your baby to sleep on his back and never on his stomach.

Dress your baby in clothes suitable for the climate and wrap him in a cool light-weight wrap. Do not overheat your baby. Do not overheat the house. You don't need to pile blankets on your baby or leave a heater on to keep his room warm. We know from experience that bumpers around cots are dangerous. Toys in the cot are dangerous too. The cot should have nothing in it other than a mattress and a clean, tightly fitted sheet, with the baby wrapped firmly down the end of the bed, a light sheet placed over him and tucked in. Nothing else is required.

Don't put a hat on your baby when he is in bed, as he can pull that down over his face. Don't put mittens on your baby, as he can bite on them, which may cause him to choke.

Smoking is also a major contributing factor to SIDS.

Many years ago, women thought it was OK to smoke during pregnancy. People also smoked in the house more, so children were raised in smoke-filled homes. Now, with new understanding of this health issue, we know that cigarette smoke or passive smoking is very dangerous, not only for babies, but for all of us.

It's important to have a smoke-free environment. Anyone close to your baby who smokes should be sent outside while they do so. Get them to wash their hands and face afterwards. One suggestion I make is to have a coat that smokers must put on outside when they smoke. This reduces the amount of smoke on the smoker's clothes. If you put a baby close to you after you've had a cigarette, the baby can still inhale some of the passive smoke.

Sleeping with your newborn baby in the bed should be discouraged. That doesn't mean that you can't have your baby in the bed while you're awake to play and have some cuddles. It's more of a concern if you are tired and you have a doona on the bed that could suffocate your baby. It's best to have your baby in a cot beside your bed or wherever you feel is safe.

Please read up on SIDS and the risks. It is a very important subject for all new parents, grandparents and carers.

Five ways for your baby to sleep safely and reduce the risk of SIDS in infancy

- Put your baby to sleep on his back, in a safe cot in your bedroom.
- Keep his head and face uncovered at all times.
- Keep the baby in a smoke-free environment before and after birth.
- Make sure he is in a safe sleeping environment both night and day.
- Breastfeed your baby.

Your post-pregnancy body

You can't compare your body before, during and after pregnancy. You do put on weight. It's quite normal, natural and healthy to gain weight during pregnancy. Most obstetricians these days don't weigh women during their pregnancy.

We don't encourage you to 'eat for two', but to eat a natural, healthy diet. Vitamin supplements are encouraged, including a multivitamin, vitamin D and folate. Iron supplements may be necessary if you are low in iron. You can continue multivitamins, vitamin D and iron while breastfeeding your baby.

Resuming exercise is a big question. Some women want to get into exercise straightaway. Remember you've just had a baby. Your body has been through a process, not just during labour, but right through pregnancy. After six weeks you can usually go back to your normal exercise program.

Don't run a marathon on your first day back at exercise. Take it slowly. A daily walk with your baby is fantastic and helps you physically and emotionally. A walk is also great for your baby so he can look at different things—the trees, birds, cars. Talk to him, explain everything to him.

Not everyone loses weight after they've had a baby. Sometimes it's the hardest weight to lose. If you're breastfeeding, you might lose weight quickly, but it's not a race. You are feeding your baby. Your body naturally needs weight to feed your baby. It's important to eat right and exercise, but do it slowly. Nothing happens overnight.

If you have had an episiotomy or tear during a vaginal birth, it's very important to take care of it. It takes six weeks for this wound to heal, so keep the area clean and dry. I suggest having a daily salt bath—simply add a handful of salt to your bath. Just being in the bath is very soothing and healing. Put a towel between your legs to dry yourself and don't rub; any rubbing will be far too painful. Put on a clean pad and underpants that are firm and supportive. This will help with pain relief. Keep ahead of your pain and continue your pain relief.

The material used to stitch an episiotomy or a tear will dissolve. It causes some anxiety to women to think that the area is open or gaping. The body is very clever. To prevent bruising, infection or a hematoma, which is a solid swelling of clotted blood, the body opens up the area to let out the collected blood. Keep the area clean and dry and it will heal by six weeks. It doesn't mean that it's not tender or sensitive, but it will have healed. Some women like to have a look at the perineal area after they've had a baby, as do some of the partners. Sometimes it's a bit frightening when you look, as the wound is open and gaping.

After a caesarean section the wound sometimes heals with the skin gaping to let the clotted or excess blood under the skin escape. We don't want blood to stay under the wound because that can cause an infection.

Always get your wound checked if it's red, sore, hot or there's any offensive smell. Keep up your pain relief and look after yourself. Don't carry heavy objects. Don't run around. Don't get back to exercise until you've seen your doctor. You need to recover from the birth. This takes six to eight weeks. Be patient with yourself.

Caring for your nipples is important when you're breast-feeding. You don't need to put any synthetic lotion on your nipples to heal them. All you need is your breast milk. Once the baby has finished sucking rub some excess breast milk on your nipples and let it dry. Mother Nature knows what to do. Trust your body. Creams, lotions, potions will not help sore nipples.

Your baby's reflexes

We talked earlier about the startle, or Moro, reflex (see page 33). Your baby also has a very strong sucking reflex. When the nipple stimulates the baby's tongue, he will suck and swallow, suck and swallow. It's a primitive urge to live, so the baby will drink and sustain life.

The baby also has the rooting reflex. If you touch the baby on the side of his face, he will turn instinctively to that side and seek out the nipple. A baby knows where to find the breast.

Babies have a stepping, or walking, reflex. If you hold a baby upright, when he has no clothes on, with his feet touching the floor, he will stand and walk along the surface with your support.

All these reflexes are highly toned when the baby is born and slowly diminish as the baby gets older.

Clicky hips

Some babies are born with clicky hips. It often happens with babies who are in the breech position, which is when the baby is born bottom or legs first, rather than head first. The baby's hips stretch into a position that causes them to become a little loose, hence clicky hips.

At six weeks, if the baby has clicky hips or any concerns with the hips, the doctor will order an ultrasound to ensure that the muscles around the hips are nice and firm and keeping them in place. Some babies require follow-up ultrasounds to ensure the hips are not still immature. Don't panic. If the hips need ongoing treatment the doctor will refer you to an orthopaedic specialist, who may prescribe a soft, flexible brace for a short period to correct the position of the hips. Each baby will need to wear the brace for a different length of time.

Skin

Rashes, birthmarks, spots and dots all cause new parents worry and anxiety. If you are concerned, have the baby checked by a medical professional. Check his temperature (it is best to use a digital thermometer under the baby's arm for a reliable reading) and also take a photo of the rash to show the doctor, as the rash can change from hour to hour.

Dry skin

Babies have very dry skin within the first six weeks. Be patient: don't put any creams or moisturisers on your baby. The dry skin goes and within weeks he will have lovely smooth skin.

Cradle cap

Cradle cap can be prevented. It's layer upon layer of dry skin, usually on the baby's head over the anterior fontanelle (the soft spot on top of the baby's head) and also between the eyebrows. It occurs in these places as most parents are worried about hurting the baby over the soft spot and washing in these places. My advice is to:

- gently rub the baby's head in a circular motion with a wet face washer when bathing him, ensuring you wash the front soft spot

- wring out a wet face washer and use it to gently rub between the baby's eyebrows a few times.

There is no need to add or rub on any oil, moisturisers or lotion onto the baby's head—these will only increase the risk of cradle cap.

Nappy rash

Babies can get nappy rash from time to time and in the early weeks it is usually due to thrush. Ensure you clean the baby's bottom gently and pat dry, then smother it in an anti-fungal baby cream. The rash will disappear in 24 hours. I don't use baby wipes on bottoms when changing a baby's nappy; instead I use warm water and cotton balls. Put your baby wipes in the nappy bag, as they are fabulous to use when you are out.

Spots and dots

Babies have lots of spots and dots on them in the first six weeks. Be patient with his skin and avoid too many lotions and potions. The spots do resolve within six to eight weeks.

Naevus flammeus or 'stork bite' mark

This mark worries lots of mums and dads. Most babies are born with this on the nape of the neck, top of the eyelids and forehead. The stork marks are pink and most babies have them. The marks usually disappear by twelve to eighteen months of age.

Mongolian blue spots

Mongolian blue spots are harmless bluish patches of skin, usually on the lower back and buttocks. They are more common in babies from Asian and African backgrounds. They do look very much like a bruise, so many mums and dads are alarmed when they first see one on their baby.

Haemangioma of infancy or 'strawberry mark'

Another name for a strawberry mark is haemangioma. They are red, raised and lumpy areas, and some are visible at birth. Most appear after one to four weeks. They get bigger before they slowly stop growing. I would advise seeing a paediatrician as there are medications that can shrink the haemangioma.

Milia

About half of all newborns will develop small white spots called milia, usually on their nose and face. They clear in weeks. Only wash with water. No cream is required.

Erythema toxicum

After a few days half of all newborns will have a normal newborn rash called *Erythema toxicum*. It won't harm your baby and the rash clears in weeks. Wash with water. No cream is required.

Baby acne

Pimples sometimes develop over a baby's face, cheeks and nose. These tend to get worse before clearing up completely at around six weeks. Wash with water. No cream is required.

Siblings and the new baby

'Who is that new baby's mum and dad?' squawked a three-year-old boy, the son of two dear clients of mine who had just welcomed their second child into the world.

His parents were so excited to have their firstborn son visit his new baby sister. Next to the new baby was a huge truck for him, with a card that said, 'To Leo, from your new baby sister Anna'.

They were knocked back into their seats when he asked them that question. In that moment, they had their first taste of the difficulties that can arise when a new child is introduced into the family.

While the parents can feel excited about giving their toddler a present from their new sibling, often the toddlers are interested in neither their new sibling nor the present. New families tend to overdo the 'present'. A toddler does not need a present from the baby to feel secure. I have seen many new trucks sitting in the corner of rooms.

Imagine if another adult moved into your home. There would be lots of questions, emotions and discussions. A toddler does not have the developmental capacity to ask questions, and the only way he can demonstrate his emotions is by screaming, hitting, crying and sometimes regressing in such things as toilet-training.

All this is normal. But there are a few basic steps to follow to help the little one—and you—cope better with the situation.

Toddlers do not have the developmental capacity to be jealous. That is a learnt behaviour. Don't push the friendship, it will happen. He needs lots of love and attention from his parents.

Here are a few basic ideas to help a sibling adjust to a newborn:

- Lots of cuddles: toddlers need attention and they need it now. This will make him feel more secure. He will get sick of the attention and eventually go and do his own thing. Constantly ask him to come to you for a cuddle rather than say 'no' to everything he does. Have a few tricks up your sleeve while you are sitting and feeding the new baby, such as a small book you can read to him, or a game you can play together. (You will understand the meaning of multiskilling.)

- While feeding the new baby, have the toddler sit next to you. Talk to him, explain what is happening.
- When the baby is crying, teach him to pat the baby gently. Tell him to kiss the baby on the top of her head. Tell him what to do because he does not know.
- Don't stress him out. Talk to him and provide reassurance. Tell him you love him.
- Maintain your daily routine. Toddlers love routine and as soon as you are home, keep it going. If he has been in child-care, keep the routine tight, on time and ongoing. Maintain daytime sleeps and the night-time routine of dinner, bath, book and bed. Keep him sleeping in his cot. This helps the toddler feel safe and secure. Remember, he needs his boundaries.

As parents we are teachers. We need to teach children what to do, but often we have unreal expectations about exactly what a toddler of two to three years is emotionally and developmentally capable of doing.

How your child learns to adapt to a new baby within the home sets his emotional pattern for how he will get on with others in his life. He can find the new situation a bit overwhelming too, and if you talk to him he will learn that you are OK. And when you are OK, he will be OK!

The household dynamics have changed forever; new parents need to recognise this and be mindful of how the toddler is coping.

Good luck, I know you will all survive. My seven older brothers and sisters did!

Miscarriage, stillborn baby or death of a newborn

We all worry about our children from the time of conception. Parenting begins then, and never leaves us. Parenting is for life. When women lose a baby through miscarriage, stillbirth or neonatal death, the grief is lonely and physically painful.

Hospital staff know how devastating loss is and are trained to comfort and support you. They know what to do about organising ministers of religion if you wish, funeral directors and the tender care of your baby.

But when you go home the nursery has no baby, and the clothes and toys you have purchased are all sad reminders of what you have lost. Everyone grieves differently. The hardest hurdle is telling people about your loss and coping with many different reactions. Some of your closest friends may not even contact you while you will be surprised by the strength of a distant friend who may have gone through the same experience.

When counselling grieving parents, I always say the death of a baby through miscarriage, stillbirth or neonatal death brings out the best and worst in people. Some people are kind and empathetic while others run a mile, not knowing what to do or say to you. There is professional help available—counselling is not to help you forget the baby you have lost, but to help you manage your grief.

If you already have children, the grief after a loss of a baby is not easier. Far too many people say to mothers, 'Oh, you are lucky as you already have children.' Women need to grieve the child they have lost.

Jed was eight weeks premature. We had the most incredible 21 days with our happy healthy Jed before he became terminally ill after suffering a catastrophic bleed on the brain (stroke). He grew his angel wings, leaving us on 13 September.

Immediately after Jed's death, what I felt was pain. Not just emotional pain, but a physical pain, as though someone had ripped a piece of my heart out. It felt like someone had poured cold water over my head and as it ran down my body it began to freeze. I was completely gutted. I felt physically sick and didn't eat for days.

It is difficult to think what the death of your child might be like. We are mourning the loss of Jed's life, but we also mourn the loss of his potential, his future and our life as a family. Tony and I had a complete incapacity to take it in. In a way, our bodies and minds stopped us taking it in because it was too awful. It felt like a kind of natural defence mechanism that kept reality at bay.

The first month was a blur and an emotional rollercoaster. Upon reflection it's nothing like a roller-coaster—rollercoasters are fun, there are highs and lows, but they only last a second.

There are no tangible words to describe Jed's death and the days to come. The grief that gripped us after the death of baby Jed is soul-deep and raw, like an exposed nerve. The pain that accompanied the loss of Jed was so intense that my body and mind retreated into an emotional haze that numbed my senses. I was in a state of shock and numbness for about eight weeks. But eventually that numbness dissipated and I carry grief's indelible mark.

They say time heals everything but at the three-month mark it honestly felt ten times harder. The initial shock is over and I am left to face the reality of saying goodbye forever.

Death, loss and grief evoke feelings of pure anger. Anger is an emotion I least expected to come across. But as time went by anger consumed me. I was angry about Jed's death, I was angry with the medical world, nurses, doctors, particular specialist doctors, I was angry that I had to return to work.

ELISE AND TONY

What is not helpful for grieving parents

- ignoring and abandoning them
- saying or doing nothing
- thinking they will 'get over it' or should have moved on by now.

What is helpful for grieving parents

- being present (even if you have no words) is so much better than being silent. It is OK to not know what to say
- acknowledging the baby as well as the profound loss rather than avoiding the subject and pretending it never happened. Remember, it is never too late to say something, or send a card or letter
- acknowledging the birthing experience and postpartum challenges parents still face without the joy of a baby
- respecting the parents' attempts to cope initially after the death of their child and then in the following days, weeks, months and years.

So much happens in the first six weeks after your baby is born, but over the next twleve months his physical and emotional development will amaze you. The baby grows and develops from a newborn to a walking, talking, active, creative toddler at twelve months of age. Enjoy the journey; love and nurture the life you have created. We have one shot at doing a fabulous job with parenting, so never underestimate how your role as a parent and teacher impacts on your baby from day one and for the rest of his life.

Week 6

Feed, play and sleep routine

Bath, bottle and bed

You guessed it: the bath, bottle and bed routine stays the same. The bath time comes back *slowly* once your baby is sleeping, from after the bottle (say 10.30 pm) until 4 to 5 am. This may take three to four months, depending on his birth weight and weight gain; usually he will be about 8 to 9 kilograms. This routine works. Don't be too eager to bring the bath back quickly as it will disturb the baby sleeping after midnight till morning and that's when you need him (and you) to be asleep. Remember he is still only six weeks old. Be aware of Google and girlfriends advising you that this is far too late to bath your baby—this routine sets you up for the next month, and the next, and the next. This is the foundation of helping a baby into a great sleeping routine.

Daytime feeds

Daytime feeds are more organised now but still you will find the baby requires lots of feeding after 6 pm. Your lactation can take until now to get established, so well done, breastfeeding is much easier from now on. You will find the baby will dictate how long he feeds. Some babies feed for 30 minutes, others for five minutes, but both are satisfied and gaining weight. This reflects how we all lactate differently, how all our children gain weight at a different rate and time so it's best not to compare with other mums and their babies.

Play

Your baby is now really capable of playing on his mat on the floor for up to 20–30 minutes between feeds. Beware of the gadgets that look like fun, including bouncers, swings, rockers, walkers, jolly jumpers, play gyms—all of these will interfere with your baby's natural and progressive development. Mother Nature wants your baby to be free and active, flat on the floor. That's where he will learn all his skills, such as rolling, grasping, doing 360-degree turns on his tummy, moving backwards and commencing to go forwards on his tummy by commando-crawling before he gets up on his hands and knees and moves forward by crawling. Then he learns to sit, not the other way around. He doesn't need to sit alone, as this will encourage him to sit in one spot and then bum-shuffle rather than do the preferred hands-and-knees crawling.

The best thing about turning six weeks old is his smile. Just when you think this is all too hard, he melts your heart with a knowing and loving smile. Now you are in love forever.

By the end of week six . . .

- The baby smiles at you for the first time.
- You feel your routine is really working well now.
- The baby is interactive and shows signs of tiredness and hunger.
- He can stay up and play for longer times.
- The baby still sleeps three to four times during the day, for 45 minutes to an hour.
- In the night-time your baby should sleep for long stretches.
- By six weeks the baby should have gained one kilo.
- If you have not breastfed you may get your period.
- You have your six-week appointment with both your obstetrician and paediatrician.
- Contraception starts again.
- You can start exercising again.

Feeding chart

Date and time	Breast (mins) Left	Breast (mins) Right	Formula (mls)	Nappy Wet	Nappy Pooey	Sleep (mins)	Comments
18-Apr-16 12:41pm	3	4	180	✓	—	105	Settled easily

Feeding chart

Date and time	Breast (mins)		Formula (mls)	Nappy		Sleep (mins)	Comments
	Left	Right		Wet	Pooey		
18-Apr-16 12:41pm	3	4	180	✓	—	105	Settled easily

Feeding chart

| Date and time | Breast (mins) | | Formula (mls) | Nappy | | Sleep (mins) | Comments |
	Left	Right		Wet	Pooey		
18-Apr-16 12:41pm	3	4	180	✓	—	105	Settled easily

10

Beyond six weeks

Your baby is going to keep changing every day, every week, month and year. No two days will be the same.

Try to make parenting a positive experience. Always talk to your baby in a positive tone. Rather than say, 'Don't do that', say 'How about we do it like this'. Your baby is already learning from you and taking in whatever you say as well as your tone.

In the first seven years of life children are sitting in imaginary wet cement and absorbing what we teach them. We teach them good from bad. We teach them to be happy and, if we're not careful, we can teach them to be sad. It is our responsibility as parents to develop happy, loving children.

There's an old saying: 'Show me the child at seven and I'll show you the man or the woman'. Whatever the age of the baby, it's our responsibility as parents, as life teachers, to promote safety and a healthy life. We can protect. We can love. We can share, and we can have a happy time. You are the voice in your child's thoughts.

I have discussed how to get your baby into a routine. The most important thing is to have your baby sleeping a good stretch overnight. That foundation will continue as your child gets older.

Babies who sleep well from birth and continue to do so may not sleep well as they get older. There are various reasons why they change their sleep habits and wake consistently overnight (see the box below). But the baby who is under six months old or weighs less than 8 kilograms needs food, so do not let him cry it out or leave him alone.

What changes babies' sleep routine

- **Teething** Some babies have a terrible time with teething, while others have a head full of teeth before you know it, with no change in their behaviour. Others may get a red-hot cheek along with runny poo that tends to nearly burn the baby's bottom, causing nappy rash.
- **Travel** A change in environment does cause a baby to change his sleep pattern. Many parents go on a holiday and it sounds great at the time . . .

- **Illness** When a baby is unwell with a cold, gastro, viral and/ or bacterial infection he wakes up frequently, disturbing his sleep.
- **Lack of activity during the day** Usually at about four months the baby tends to start waking up, maybe before midnight and, at times, every two hours after that. Babies need to be really active on the floor during the day. Remember: Food + activity = sleep.
- **A dummy** After six months the baby often wakes up, looking for a dummy. The mum goes in and out of the nursery all night putting it back in, setting up a broken sleep pattern.

Passive settling

Do you need your baby to go back to sleep? No time for sleep school? Here is the only way to successfully get your babies back to sleep. It's called controlled crying and everyone has a breakdown over it, thinking they are going to cause their child long-term harm, but believe me, a child waking up three to seven times a night will do your parenting more harm than controlled crying. More to the point, what is the effect of long-term sleep deprivation on the baby and parents?

So let's call it passive settling so it doesn't feel like we are standing over our child 'controlling him' while he is 'crying his eyes out'. I have successfully taught 'passive settling' for over 33 years and, in fact, used it with my own son when he was eight months old and waking every few hours after a bout of gastro.

Babies need to learn a skill before they can accomplish it. So if they are waking constantly overnight they need to learn to go back to sleep. The aim of passive settling is for the baby to go back to sleep by himself, but for that to happen you must follow a strict process. Over the years many people have told me they have tried 'controlled crying' many times and it never works. If it hasn't worked, it probably wasn't done properly.

Passive settling allows the baby to go to sleep, with the parent checking and reassuring him at intervals, which increase in duration, until the baby goes to sleep by himself.

My rules with passive settling are as follows. The baby MUST:

- be over six months of age and/or over 8 kilograms in weight
- show NO signs of illness
- be in his own home and cot
- not be about to travel on holidays for the next few weeks.

The method

Ensure the baby has had dinner and a bath by 6 pm. I try not to give babies too much milk before bed before the first session of passive settling as some babies may vomit; that will cause distress for the baby and more work for you. Offer lots of fluids during the day and a small drink before bed. If the baby is teething give him the recommended dose of Panadol per weight and age. This ensures he is pain-free and also helps you not to stress out that the baby may be in pain.

Once the baby is ready for bed, dress him appropriately and place him in a sleeping bag. No sheets, pillows or blankets in the cot. Kiss him goodnight, tell him how much you love him then put him into bed and walk out the door.

That is probably the hardest thing to do—to leave the baby in the cot and walk out the door. Remember he is safe.

Then I suggest you get your phone, turn the timer on and let it tick over for two minutes. When a baby is crying, they can seem like two very, very long minutes. It's best not to stand outside the door listening to him cry. Have a walk around the house, make a cup of tea, do something to distract yourself.

After the two minutes are up, go in to the baby and reassure him, saying the same thing, 'Good night darling, time for bed, good boy. Mummy is here and I will be coming back. It's time to go to sleep, that's a good boy.'

I suggest you don't stay in the baby's room for a long time because that will stress the baby and yourself. Stay for about 15–30 seconds, reassuring the baby, and then leave the room.

Many years ago we used to pick up the baby, hold him to settle and then put him back down to bed. The process certainly took longer that way and seemed to aggravate the crying process. Reassuring the baby in his cot is a lot quicker and more efficient. Once you have left the room, set the timer for four minutes and go through the same process.

The sequence you need to go through is 2-, 4-, 6-, 8-, 10- and 15-minute intervals. If the baby is still crying after 15 minutes go in and reassure him every 15 minutes.

I must say in my experience it's pretty rare for a baby to still be crying every 15 minutes. I find that between the four- and six-minute mark there tends to be a lull in the baby's crying, just for a few seconds. This is when you start to feel you've nearly achieved your goal.

All babies do this differently. Some take only half an hour, while others seem to take hours. When the baby stops crying and goes to sleep you really won't believe the silence. High-fives all around!

When the baby is finally asleep, leave him. If you have a monitor and look at him, don't worry if he is up one end of the cot; just leave him. Remember to ensure there are no toys, sheets, pillows or blankets in the cot before beginning this process.

The next time the baby wakes up, wait for two minutes before going in to him. There is a slight chance that he may go back to sleep but, if after two minutes he hasn't, go in and start the process again. You do not need to give the baby Panadol. I find during this part of the process the baby may settle quicker. High-fives again!

Depending on the baby's age, if he goes to bed at 6 pm and has slept through until 4 or 5 o'clock, I would definitely feed him. Then he will go back to sleep for another few hours.

Passive settling really works and you need to give it a go if you have a child who is waking constantly overnight. Constant patting and shushing of a baby in a cot only distresses both the baby and the mother and, in my experience, doesn't work. The intervals between going in to the baby can seem long, but you need to be prepared. You need your partner's support. If you stop the process, feed the baby and 'break the rules', you will need to start again. Thus, once you start this technique you need to be strong and continue until the baby is asleep.

The next day you need to continue in the same way for the daytime sleeps too. At sleep time put the baby down into the cot and start the process again, leaving him to cry for two minutes, four minutes, six minutes, and so on. You will find that babies get the message very quickly and learn how to go to sleep.

It's important that both you and your partner are consistent when doing passive settling. If one of you isn't dedicated, it won't work. Once you give in you will have to start again from scratch.

If the baby has a dummy at this stage and you are still settling him with it, you need to throw out the dummy and settle him without it. It will be more successful. Also if you are feeding the baby to sleep either by the breast or the bottle, you need to put the baby into bed awake. You will find that he will not need to be fed to sleep after passive settling has been done.

For some babies passive settling takes only a couple of days, while other babies can take up to seven. But he won't be crying hard from the first time you did it. What I find down the track is that the baby may wake up at, say, 2 in the morning and have just a little bit of a grizzle for a couple of minutes and before you're up and out of bed, he's put himself back to sleep. That is the success of passive settling.

Remember most babies have a little ritual before they go to sleep. Some babies grizzle, some roll around, some babies sing, some laugh and some have a cry and carry on, but they do go to sleep. The baby waking every couple of hours up to seven to ten times a night is not normal, for you or your baby, and you need to get him back to sleeping overnight.

If you feel you can't do it any longer and you want to go in and pick your baby up, do it.

Not everyone agrees with passive settling, but not everyone has seen the success I have, with so many happy babies and even happier and rested parents. Each sleeping issue is unique, with various solutions, but I can at least give you some sensible advice.

Introduction of solid foods

The recommended age for introducing solid foods to an infant's diet has varied over the years. In infants up to six months, breast milk and formula are the ideal foods to meet all nutritional requirements.

Introducing solids always causes a bit of anxiety. You do not want dinnertime to be full of anxiety so there is no hurry. If your baby refuses food one day, leave it for a few days, then start over again. It will happen, but you need the baby to be ready.

Parents think their baby wants food at a very early age, as he is watching them eat, following food to their mouths. It's because he is visually excited by any colour and movement.

Your baby has a sucking reflex, a primitive reflex to live. Your baby is also born with the extrusion reflex. You may notice he sticks his tongue in and out. Many parents (we all do) think their baby is so smart, copying them poking their tongues out, but this is again another primitive reflex your baby has been born with—to push anything hard away from his mouth. Mother Nature has hardwired the baby to protect him from hard and possibly dangerous objects or food that he is not yet able to chew and swallow.

The extrusion reflex is normal. It does not mean your baby doesn't like food. He cannot swallow anything hard, and it's all about sucking at this stage of his life. When the extrusion reflex disappears in a healthy baby, he is able to move food to the back of his mouth and swallow safely. This is when your baby is ready for solids.

There are many new and varied fads about introducing food to babies. Believe me, child development has not changed.

The physical characteristics that allow for the introduction of solid foods to the infant at around four to six months of age include:

- renal function, which allows the baby to handle an increased load associated with solids
- digestive enzymes, which mature at around six months
- immune factors, when the intestinal defence mechanism of the gut develops fully
- the disappearance of the extrusion reflex at around four to six months so the baby is able to move food to the back of the mouth and swallow safely
- improved head control that enables the baby to swallow more easily when sitting.

In deciding when to begin solids, consider your baby's readiness and interest in food. The development of feeding skills for various age groups describes the child's ability to manage the change in textures from liquids to solids. Newborns suck and swallow fluids. In the early months you may notice that your baby is dribbling a lot—this is because he cannot keep the dribble in his mouth. As the baby grows and develops he learns to keep saliva in his mouth.

By three months your baby will have an increased range of movement of mouth and lips, and better head control. At around six months he will put his fingers in his mouth, and move his tongue up and down with better jaw and lip control.

At nine months he will reach for the spoon and be interested in self-feeding. By twelve months he will be mobile, interactive and able to use a cup. He will often eat independently, chewing lumps well. Let the natural developmental process happen.

I suggest starting with food that is soft, safe and clean. Rice cereal is an ideal food to introduce first. Mix a teaspoon of rice cereal with some breast milk or formula. Offer the food to the baby. You may see some funny faces. If the baby refuses the first time, try again the next day. This is new to you both. Take your time and don't hurry as meal times are meant to be relaxing and stress-free.

Babies do not need a gourmet menu. Keep it simple, soft, clean and fresh. Once the baby has had a few days of rice cereal introduce some stewed apples at lunchtime. Continue this for another few days. Then introduce some sweet potato at dinnertime.

So now you have a plan: rice cereal for breakfast, stewed apples for lunch and mashed sweet potato for dinner. As the days and weeks go by add new foods. Again, start with a teaspoon of food and gradually increase the amount over the following days and weeks. Only offer one food at a time.

Begin with runny soft foods and smooth fruit and vegetables. The introduction of solid foods generally begins with iron-enriched infant cereal. Vegetables, fruits, meats, poultry and fish are then added gradually, one food at a time, and in small amounts.

Increase the range and quantity of foods you offer as your baby moves towards twelve months of age.

Small amounts of cow's milk in foods such as breakfast cereal, yoghurt, cheese and custards, as part of a mixed, nutrient-dense diet, are suitable from around 7 to 8 months. By the end of the first year an infant should be consuming a wide variety of family foods, having progressed from purees or mashes to foods that are chopped into small pieces.

It is not advisable to give babies under two years old honey because of the potential risk of *Clostridium botulism*. Also avoid whole nuts due to the risk of inhalation and choking.

Some general hints

- Offer minced meats and chicken from 6 to 7 months.
- Introduce other cereals from nine months.

- Give small amounts of cow's milk in custard, yoghurt and cereal from 7 to 8 months.
- Try foods that may cause allergy, such as egg white or peanut butter, after 10 to 12 months.
- Avoid small hard foods such as nuts and uncooked vegetables, due to the risk of choking.
- Be prepared for the mess as your baby learns to eat.
- Stay with your baby when he is eating, and sit him with the family at meal times to watch and learn feeding skills.
- Expect to see a change in bowel habits (and smell) when your baby starts eating foods other than milk.
- Fruit juice is not required for infants as it is very high in sugar.
- If you have a dog, he will love food time with your baby, who will throw him a perfect snack on the floor three times a day!

Key points to remember for your new baby

- Babies are primitive.
- Babies are hardwired to live, not hardwired to starve.
- Their sucking reflex is the strongest reflex so they can live.
- Babies can't be sick and well at the same time.
- Babies need attachment from their mother, and they love to be held close; this will not 'spoil' them.

- Talking, holding, touching and kissing are all part of initial and ongoing attachment. `
- You can't overfeed your baby, but you can underfeed him.
- New babies are very noisy, usually at night time.
- Babies grunt, go red in the face, squirm and pass wind in their sleep—it's normal.
- Babies are sleepy at birth and gradually wake up, having more alert time.
- Lactation is a given after birth, and formula will not interfere with your lactation as long as you continue to breastfeed before giving formula.
- When babies sleep well overnight under the age of six months they don't sleep much during the day. Often three 45-minute naps are all they are capable of.
- Respond to your baby rather than looking for 'signs' learnt in a book.
- Babies can stay up longer than you think.
- They don't get overtired, as they will fall asleep if they need sleep.

So it's over to you!

It's up to you to love and be present in the life of your child. May your voice always be positive and encouraging, may your kisses be frequent and loving, your arms always around your child to comfort and calm. For every milestone your baby reaches, celebrate with him. Tell him how much you love him every day, many times, and use his name—everyone loves the sound of their name.

Enjoy parenting. It's not always easy, but it is always rewarding!

Seeking help

For miscarriage, stillbirth and newborn death support

SANDS

National office
Level 2b, 818 Whitehorse Road,
Box Hill, Victoria, 3128
Tel: (03) 9895 8700
Email: support@sands.org.au
Web: www.sands.org.au

Queensland
Tel: (07) 3254 3422
Email: admin@sandsqld.com
Web: www.sandsqld.org.au

South Australia
Tel: 0417 681 642
Email: info@sandssa.org.au
Web: www.sandssa.org.au

Tasmania
Tel: 0415 127 464
Email: tasmania@sands.org.au
Web: www.sandstas.org.au

Victoria
Tel: (03) 9874 5400
Email: victoria@sands.org.au
Web: www.sandsvic.org.au

Western Australia
Tel: 0424 340 115
Email: adminwa@sands.org.au
Web: www.sandswa.org.au

Parenting helplines

Grandcare (information service for grandparents)
Tel: 1800 008 323

Karitane Careline
Tel: 1300 227 464

Maternal and Child Health Line
Tel: 13 22 29

Ngala Helpline
1800 111 546 (STD callers) or (08) 9368 9368

Parentline ACT
Tel: (02) 6287 3833

Parentline NSW
Tel: 1300 1300 52

Parentline Queensland and Northern Territory
Tel: 1300 301 300

Parent Helpline South Australia
Tel: 1300 364 100

Parentline Tasmania
Tel: 1300 808 178

Parentline Victoria
Tel: 13 22 89

Parenting WA Line
Tel: 1800 654 432 (STD callers) or (08) 6279 1200

13 HEALTH
Web: www.health.qld.gov.au/13health/
Tel: 13 43 25 84

Tresillian Parent Helpline
Tel: 1300 272 736
(1300 2 Parent)

General helplines

Alcohol Drug Information
Service (ADIS)
Tel: 1800 422 599,
(02) 9361 8000 (Sydney metro)

Child Care Access Hotline
Tel: 1800 670 305, 133 677
(TTY service for people with a
hearing/speech impairment)

Child Wise National Child
Abuse Helpline
Tel: 1800 99 10 99

Family Relationship Advice Line
Tel: 1800 050 321

Health Direct Australia (not
available in Victoria or
Queensland)
Tel: 1800 022 222

Kids Helpline
Tel: 1800 55 1800

Lifeline
Tel: 13 11 14

Medicare
Tel: 132 011

Mensline Australia (support
and referral to specialist men's
services)
Tel: 1300 78 99 78

National Breastfeeding Helpline
Tel: 1800 MUM 2 MUM (or
1800 686 268)

National Poisons Information
Centre
Tel: 13 11 26

National Sexual Assault,
Domestic Family Violence
Counselling Service
Tel: 1800 RESPECT, or
1800 737 732

Playgroup Australia
Tel: 1800 171 882

Sane Australia Helpline
Tel: 1800 187 263

Acknowledgements

When Claire Kingston contacted me from Allen & Unwin and asked if I was interested in writing a book about parenting it really was a dream come true. Thank you, Claire, and all at Allen & Unwin for your support and faith in me, my passion for new parents and babies. To Foong Ling Kong, editor and an amazingly skilled, passionate and caring person who has held my shaking hand and patiently guided me. As professionals and mothers, both you and Claire knew the value of a book like this for new parents. Thank you for being so supportive and patient with me. Thank you to Sarah Baker for her expertise in the final run home. Sarah, you are amazing. Thank you for your calm words and guidance.

My love and thanks to all my patients who have allowed me to not only share their birth experiences but also trusted me with their babies, listened to my advice and allowed me to be the voice in their head during the most vulnerable and emotional time of their lives.

The best life teachers I had were my parents, Doreen and Jack Curtin, and I know they would be so proud of this book and me. Mum, a tower of strength, taught me more about parenting than the textbooks (her words), and Dad provided me with a sense of humour and the courage to stand up and be myself. Both Mum and Dad taught me the meaning of love and commonsense when applied to parenting. Together they were amazing people—parents who raised me to be loving, strong, independent, courageous and passionate.

My absolutely fabulous son Lachlan Curtin-Corr knows more about childbirth and breastfeeding than the average young man, and he is the love that fills my heart. Without him my life would never have been as loving, adventurous and fulfilled, or my career as exciting or driven. He has made parenting so much fun and I have learnt so much from him. Dannie Corr, loving dad to Lachlan, and Bella Arnott-Hoare, partner to my son, have both been so encouraging about this book. Thank you all for your love and support.

To the amazing Clare O'Brien, my schoolfriend and still my bestie, even though she lives in New York. She has been my friend, confidant and support with this book. Clare has been present in my life for what seems like forever. When we were at school she wanted to live in New York and I wanted to be a midwife. Dreams do come true. Clare, thank you so much for always being there for me.

To Dr Brendan Chan, thank you for your advice and for being a breath of fresh air in the world of paediatrics. All new mothers need a kind and caring doctor like you to look after their baby.

Thank you also to my friends Joe Farago, Diana Korevaar, Dimitra Spalas, Claire West, Emily Crawford, Kylie Grogan and Bridie Standford for being so supportive and encouraging throughout this journey. Individually you have given me the strength and courage to put one foot in front of the other when it's been tough.

I have been fortunate to work with my friend, obstetrician Dr Len Kliman, for more than 30 years. He has had an immense impact on me both professionally and personally, and also safely delivered our son Lachlan. He has constantly supported me with my passion to care for women in labour and the postnatal period, to stand up for our patients who did not have a strong voice in the community, and most importantly, gave me the strength and courage to ignore my critics. And through his genius he taught me everything I know about obstetrics. He gave me a once-in-a-lifetime chance to create an independent role as an MCH nurse within his practice that allowed me to be creative and work one on one with all our new parents on childbirth and parenting, and support them by providing excellent continuity of care.

Last but by no means least, my love and thanks to the fabulous Rebecca Judd, a wonderfully kind and generous woman, a motivated professional and a loving mum who has the courage and commonsense to balance parenting and a busy work life . . . and does both brilliantly. Bec was a 'model patient' and listened to everything I advised with her children Oscar and Billie. Bec also gave me an opportunity to write on her blog 'Rebecca Judd Loves', which has given me a voice in the social media community and access to many more mums and dads around Australia and the world. Bec, you are a star! Thank you.

midwifecath.com.au
thefirst6weeks@gmail.com

Index

A

acne, baby 242
African women 61, 158
afterbirth pains 34
alcohol, education about 24
allergies 62; *see also* cow's milk, protein
    allergy
amniotic fluid 19
anger 11, 211
    grieving process, in 247
ankyloglossia 47; *see also* tongue-tie
antidepressant medication 212, 215
anxiety 158, 162, 191, 210–17, 230
    medication to treat 211
Apgar, Dr Virginia 31
Apgar score 31, 32
areolas 71–2, 74
armpits, bathing 120
attachment
    breastfeeding *see* breastfeeding
    mother and baby 8, 205–7, 268–9
Australian Institute of Health and
    Welfare 67
Australian safety standards
    cot 14
    pram 13

B

baby
    acne 242
    belly button 52–3
    blank canvas 4
    crying *see* crying babies
    dribbling 266
    facial expression 158

falling from change table 14
good routine for 2
healthy 1, 39, 49–52
hours after birth 31
hungry 43, 44–5, 62, 63, 69, 70, 76,
    110, 149
individual, as 147, 156
items baby doesn't need 198
jaundice 43, 45–6
key points to remember 268
liver 106
low-weight at term 46–7
making babies cold 64
needs of 5
noisy 2, 49–52
overfeeding 62, 76, 110, 119, 128,
    269
own person, as 3
pimples 242
rolling 196
routine 7
skin 239
sleeping *see* sleep of baby
smiles 251, 252
sucking 69, 71–3
talking to 59, 173, 208, 209, 256
things not to worry about 5
things to worry about 5
underfeeding 62, 110, 128, 269
unwell 43
'visual fixation' 59
waking 60
walking 196
weight 108
well 39

baby (*continued*)
  what not to do 137
baby blues 123, 210
baby capsules 13, 19, 57
baby gym 142, 196, 251
baby massage 143
baby monitors 15
bassinet 14
bath, bottle and bed (BBB) routine 4,
    60–1, 100, 129–32, 147
  week 1 118–19
  week 2 150
  week 3 174
  week 4 199
  week 5 218
  week 6 250
bathing baby 119–20, 133–6
  6 pm, at 129, 130, 132, 137, 147,
    260
  10 pm, at 129, 132, 136, 138
  soap 135
baths 15
  baby crying in 135
  frequency 129, 134
belly button 52–3
birth
  advice before 11
  bodily changes for 10
  distressed babies at 28
  filming 28
  first hour after 30
  focusing on 3
  news of 29
  recovery from 2, 35
  watching 27
birth centres 20, 25
blood clots 34
blood group card 17, 18
blood loss after birth 33
blood sugar level
  newborn, of 44
bottle-feeding
  organisation 97, 101
  technique 98
bottles 70, 97–9
  buying 14
  complementary feeding with 70
  early in life 90
  making bottles 101–2
  refusal of 91, 98, 104, 159, 161
  teats on 14
  tongue-tie babies 48
  washing 97

bouncer 142, 198, 251
bowels
  babies' bowel actions 105–6, 268
  mother, of, week 1 122
  opening 55
bra
  breastfeeding, for 16, 88
  underwires 16
breast(s)
  cabbage leaves 75, 84, 86, 88
  engorgement 2, 16, 35, 63, 82–3
  enlarging, 16
  expressing 21, 61, 68, 71, 74, 78, 82,
    89, 90–4
  managing engorged breasts 86–9
  massaging 75, 84
  pumps 21, 78, 89, 91, 100, 105
  refusing 98, 104, 161
  sore 75
  surgery 68–9
'breast milk jaundice' 45
breastfeeding 3, 9, 65–70
  attaching baby 21, 45, 49, 68, 71, 72,
    74, 91, 185
  bra 16, 88
  demand, on 70
  establishing 2, 68
  first feed 38
  hormones released 33
  incorrect latch 62
  long-term 185
  pethidine, effects of 24
  premature babies 94
  statistics about 67
  survey about 67
  teaching about 63, 91
  twelve months or more, for 67
  twenty-point guide 73–4
  twins 184
  uterus involution and 34
  week 6 250–1
  women choosing not to 99
  World Health Organization (WHO)
    65–6, 70
breathing difficulties 43, 45
breech position 28, 238
Brown, Professor Brené 6
Buddhism 211
burping 50, 148–9

C
cabbage leaves 75, 84, 86, 88
caesarean section 10, 31

elective 23
  multiple births 182, 185
  paediatrician at 39
  pain relief 35
  recovering from 35
  scar 152, 176
  wound 36, 236
case, packing 17
Cath's wrap 15, 33, 134, 138–9
Chan, Dr Brendan 41
change table 14
checklist
  before baby arrives 17
check-up, six week 230–1
childbirth
  blood loss following 33
  bodily changes for 10
  complications in 22
  distressed babies at 28
  drug-free 25
  filming 28
  first hour after 30
  pain relief 22–5
  psychological impact 210
  recovery after 35
  watching 27
childcare, organising 17
cleanliness, basic need for 5
Clostridium botulism 267
clothes
  buying 12
  changes of 15, 16
  hospital, taking baby clothes to 16, 18
  old 15
colic 62, 110, 112, 165
colostrum 21, 38, 45, 62
  expressing 91
congenital abnormalities 43
constipation 2
  breastfed babies 106
  pain relief and 36
  pregnancy, in 53
contraception 230, 252
controlled crying 258–9; see also passive
  settling
cots 13–14
  Australian safety standards 14
  SIDS guidelines 232–3
  things in 233
cow's milk
  introducing 267
  protein allergy 2, 106, 107, 115, 128,
    186

cradle cap 134, 239–40
crawling 195, 196, 251
  hand-and-knee 197
crying babies 2, 4, 65, 72, 111–17, 158,
    166
  bath, during 135
  birth, at 27–8
  controlled crying 258–9; see also
    passive settling
  driving with baby 114
  hungry babies 110, 149
  normal part of development 111
  periods of crying 111
  reasons for 128
  shushing 145, 146, 262
  survival tips 115–16
cuddles
  baby, for 180
  siblings, for 243
cultural confinement 229

D
daytime activity, lack of 258
daytime feeds
  week 1 120–1
  week 2 151
  week 3 174–5
  week 4 199
  week 5 218
  week 6 250
death of newborn 245–9
  help for 271
depression 191, 210–17, 230
  medication 211, 215
  mindfulness techniques 211
  partners, in 215
development
  first six weeks, in 229
  growing baby 193
  individual process 156
  natural and progressive 251
  normal 181, 194–7
diabetes
  multiple births 182, 185
diabetic mothers 43, 44
doctor
  compatibility with 22
  listening to 11
dream feed 132, 133, 137
driving home 58
dummies 76, 110, 121, 157, 163, 170,
    258
  passive settling and 263

E
ears, washing behind 119
emotions 10, 11–12, 157, 210, 215
  highs and lows 10
  mindfulness 211
  raw and uncontrollable 2
empathy 7
epidurals 23, 24
  myths about 26
  reasons for having 25–6
  side-effects 26
episiotomy 24, 25, 35, 36, 152, 176, 236
Erythema toxicum 241
exercise, resuming 235, 252
extrusion reflex 264–5
eye contact 119, 209

F
family helpers 225
fear 11
  childbirth, of 213
  parenting, in 6
feed, play, sleep (FPS) 145
  boys and girls 146
feeding aversion 90
feeding baby 61
  daytime feeds *see* daytime feeds
  dream feed 132, 133, 137
  feeding aversion 159–63
  hungry babies 110
  making babies cold and uncomfortable 64
  newborn babies 147, 150
  overfeeding 62, 76, 110, 119, 128, 269
  overnight 131
  partners bottle feeding 68
  regular feeding 76
  rollover feed 132, 133, 137
  underfeeding 62, 110, 128, 269
  undressing babies 64, 65
  week 5 205
fingernails 149
first six weeks
  beyond six weeks 256
  changing baby in 229
  confusion during 2, 8
  enjoying 3
  happiness of 2
  importance of 1
  organisation during 3
  parenting in 187
  'things' happening 2
floor play 141–2

foetal distress in labour 23
foetal monitoring 23
fontanelles 41, 134, 239
food
  babies' need for 62–5, 195, 204
  basic need for 5, 8
  honey 267
  nuts 267
  solid, introduction of 264–8
Food Standards Australia New Zealand 101
forceps delivery 24
formula 40, 62, 63, 66, 74, 76, 97–9
  best 104
  buying 14
  changing 97
  consent forms, in hospital 62
  FAQs 103–4
  little babies 44
  myths about 101
  organisation 101
  preparing 103
  small top-ups 61
  supplementary feeding 44
  top-ups 61, 69, 89, 90, 95, 100, 110, 151, 218
  warnings on tins of 101
frequency of urine 53
furniture, buying 12

G
gastric reflux 2, 7, 50, 51–2, 62, 111, 115, 121, 128, 148, 160, 165–8, 171, 175
  treatment 170
gastroenteritis 107
gavage tube 44, 96
GBS status 17, 18
gifts 15
grandparents 224–8
  helping 228
grief
  grieving parents 248
  miscarriage or death of newborn 245–9
Group B streptococcus 17
growth chart 109
  percentiles 109
gut feelings 8

H
haemangioma 241
haemorrhoids 35, 53

INDEX

hand-to-mouth reflex 72
headaches 53
healthy life, promoting 256
heartburn 53, 165
helplines 272–3
hepatitis B injection 31
heroin 23
hiccups 50, 148–9
hips, clicky 238
home births 20, 22
hormonal changes 53, 210, 213
hospitals 20–1
  1970s, in 21
  baby clothes for 16, 18
  choosing 22
  conflicting advice in 54
  costs of 63
  leaving 57
  length of stay 21, 63
  partners sleeping over in 54
  things you'll need in 18
  what to take to 17
hungry babies 43, 44–5, 62, 63, 69, 70,
  76, 110, 128, 149

I
ice packs 37
immunisations 2, 231–2
  commencement 31
  currency 56
insomnia 53
instincts, trusting 8, 55
intussusception 106
IVF 181

J
jaundice 43, 45–6, 120
jealousy 243
jumper 142, 195, 251

K
Kliman, Dr Len 213
Korevaar, Dr Diana 190, 210

L
labour 3
  differences between individuals 20
  foetal distress in 23
  inducing 23
  partner support during 26–7
  persons present as 26
lactation 21, 61, 66, 69, 70, 71, 82–3,
  90, 93, 95, 218, 250, 269

bodily changes 10
brain function 61, 69
breast surgery and 69
established 205
medications 100
laxatives 55
letdown reflex 69, 83
love 2, 8, 55
  babies' need for 5, 8, 196, 204
  children learning 208
  loving your baby 119, 157, 208, 257,
    270
  what our own parenting teaches us,
    about 207
low-weight babies, feeding 46

M
mastitis 2, 75, 83–6, 95
maternal and child health nurse (MCH)
  feeding aversion, help with 163
  home visit 122, 144
  service 144
meconium 38, 105
medication, for depression 212, 215
meditation 213
midwives
  compatibility with 22
  listening to 11
  well trained 63
milia 241
milk 62, 66
  amount of 73, 89
  coming in 16, 21, 63, 69, 71, 73
  expressed, using 105
  expressing 21, 61, 68, 71, 74, 78, 82,
    89, 90–4, 103
  leaking or dripping 83
  not enough 89
  sharing 100
mindfulness 211, 213
miscarriage 245–9
  help for 271
mittens 16, 72–3, 149, 233
Mongolian blue spots 241
Moro reflex 33, 139, 149, 237
mother and child
  attachment 205–7
  bond 2, 180, 209
multiple births 181–2
muscle cramps
  pregnancy, in 53

N

naevus flammeus 240
nappies, wet 162
nappy bag 16
nappy changing 14
    first 38
nappy rash 240
    teething and 257
narcotic analgesics 23, 25
'naughty' babies 114
nausea 53
necks, smelly 119
neuroplasticity 211, 216–17
newborn 10
    appearance of 27
    baby check 40
    blood sugar level 44
    crying 27–8
    death of 245–9
    examination 40–3
    facts about 43
    feeding 147, 150
    first bowel motion 105
    first hour after birth 30
    hours after birth 31
    low-weight at term 46–7
    mixing up days and nights 60, 119,
        120, 147
    mucus in mouth/throat 31
    physical abnormalities 40
    primitive reflexes 33, 55, 72, 138,
        139, 264
    rash 241
    sleepy 64
    stomach size 62
nipples 71–2, 77–9, 82
    bleeding 2
    breast milk on 75, 76, 237
    caring for 237
    confusion about 98, 104
    flat or inverted 73, 76, 77, 78
    length 73, 77
    letdown reflex 69, 83
    nipple pain 79–80
    nipple shield 48, 73, 76, 77–9, 82
    sore and cracked 2, 61, 76, 77

O

obesity 108
oxytocin 25, 69

P

pacifiers 70; *see also* dummies

paediatrician
    examination of baby 39, 40–3
pain 2
    afterbirth 34
    baby in 162
    breastfeeding, during 79–80
    nipple pain 79–80
    postnatal 35
    removing 24
pain relief
    caesarean, following 35
    childbirth, in 22–5
    constipation and 36
parenthood, journey of 8
parenting
    approaches to 4
    enjoying 270
    fear in 6
    feelings about 1, 3
    helplines 272–3
    life as new parent 210
    parents as teachers 158, 173, 244,
        249, 256
    patience 117, 136
    personal development and 197
    positive experience 256
    preconceived ideas about 157
    psychological impact 210
    slight worry, feeling of 1
    style 3
paronychia 149
partners
    anxiety and depression 215
    bottle feeding 68
    cutting the cord 52
    hospital, sleeping over in 54
    labour, support during 26–7
    support 53
    watching the birth 27
passive settling 258–64
    method 260–4
patience 117, 136
perineum
    appearance of 36, 236
    healing 34
    recovery 36
pethidine 23–4
placenta
    expelling 61, 69
play 141
    feed, play, sleep (FPS) 145
    floor play 141–2
    week 1 121–2

week 2 151
week 3 175
week 4 200
week 5 219
week 6 251
poo 105, 159
  black, red and white 106
  blood in 107
  teething and 257
postnatal care
  changes in 21, 22
postnatal depression 160, 212, 230
pram
  Australian safety accreditation 13
  buying 13
  walking baby in 200, 235
  wraps for 198, 200, 209
pre-eclampsia
  multiple births 182, 185
pregnancy
  bodily changes 10, 53
  eating during 235
  post-pregnancy body 235
  psychological impact 210
  scans during 1
premature babies 43, 44
  breastfeeding 94–5
  expressing milk 91, 92, 94
  twins 181, 185
psychological impact 210

R
red poo 106
reflexes 72, 237
  extrusion 264–5
  hand-to-mouth 72
  Moro 33, 139, 149, 237
  oral/anal 159
  primitive 33, 55, 72, 138, 139, 264
  rooting 122, 237
  startle 33, 139, 140, 237
  stepping or walking 237
  sucking 71–3, 237, 264, 268
reflux see gastric reflux
rollover feed 132, 133, 137
rooting reflex 122
routine 172–3, 257
  babies, for 7
  bath, bottle and bed (BBB) 4, 60–1,
    100, 129–32, 147
  changing 61
  establishing 7
  full daily routine 147

ongoing 204
six-month-old babies 147
toddlers, for 244

S
safety, promoting 256
salt baths 21, 37, 236
security 180
  basic need for 5, 156, 157
  siblings, for 243
  wrapping and 173
self-settling 208
serum bilirubin (SBR) 46
settling, passive 258
sex
  birth, following 34
  resuming sexual relations 230
shame 6, 7
siblings 242–5
  security 243
SIDS see sudden infant death syndrome
singlets 15, 18
sitting position 195, 197, 251
six-week check-up 230–1
skin
  baby acne 242
  cradle cap 239–40
  dry skin 239
  Erythema toxicum 241
  haemangioma 241
  milia 241
  Mongolian blue spots 241
  nappy rash 240
  naevus flammeus 240–1
  rashes and birthmarks 239
  spots and dots 240
  'stork bite' mark 240–1
  'strawberry mark' 241
sleep deprivation 7, 60, 118, 146, 157,
    171, 189, 190, 191, 210, 214
  first six weeks, in 2
  long-term, effect of 258
sleep of baby 118
  baby not sleeping well 171
  backs, on 139
  changing sleep patterns 257
  days after birth 39, 60
  daytime sleep 147
  differences for every baby 146, 147
  feed, play, sleep (FPS) 145
  illness and 258
  newborn babies 147
  parent's bed, in 157

sleep of baby (*continued*)
   ritual before falling asleep 263
   'sleep schools' 146
   sleeping bag 139
   teething and 257
   travel and 257
   tummy, on 138, 140
   weight and 128, 129
sleep of parents 131
   newborn in bed with 234
smile of baby 251, 252
smoking 226, 233
soft cheese 24
solid food, introduction of 264–8
special care nursery 44
'spoiled' babies 175, 180, 208, 209, 268
spoiling yourself 224
startle reflex 33, 139, 140, 237
steriliser
   electric 14, 97
   microwave 14
   unpacking 19
stillborn baby 245–9
   help for 271
'stork bite' mark 240–1
strawberry mark 241
stress 191, 214
   response 12
sucking 69
   blister 72
   reflex 71–3
sudden infant death syndrome (SIDS)
      guidelines 138–9, 225, 232–4
swings 141, 198, 251

T
teachers, parents as 158, 173, 244, 249,
      256
teats 14, 70
   washing 97
teething 257, 260
thrush 80
toddlers
   jealousy 243
   siblings 242–4
tongue-tie 47–9
toys 141, 142, 194
   baby gyms 142, 196, 198, 251
   cot, in 233
travel 257
tummy time 143, 181, 200, 205
twins 181–93

U
ultrasounds 23
umbilical cord
   cord stump 52
   cutting 28, 52
UNICEF 70
urine 106
uterus
   breastfeeding and 34
   involution 33

V
vaginal birth 10, 20, 35
varicose veins 53
vernix 27, 120
visitors, controlling 55–7
'visual fixation' 59
vitamin K 31
vitamin supplements 235
vomiting 53, 149, 168

W
walkers 142, 198, 251
walking baby 200, 235
warmth
   babies' need for 196, 204
   basic need for 5
waters breaking 19
wee 106
week 1 118–23
week 2 127–52
week 3 156–76
week 4 180–200
week 5 204–19
week 6 223–52
weight 108
   average weight gain 108
   full daily routine, for 147
   gaining 128, 137, 205
   sleep and 128, 129
white noise 51, 114, 198
white poo 106
whooping cough 56, 226
wind 50, 110, 123, 148–9, 159, 165
witching hour 199
wound
   infection 2
wraps 33, 65, 73
   birth, after 38
   Cath's wrap 15, 33, 134, 138–9
   muslin 15, 139